50 American Pastry Recipes for Home

By: Kelly Johnson

Table of Contents

- Classic Apple Pie
- Blueberry Cobbler
- Chocolate Chip Cookies
- New York Cheesecake
- Lemon Bars
- Red Velvet Cupcakes
- Pecan Pie
- Key Lime Pie
- Boston Cream Pie
- Banana Bread
- Peanut Butter Cookies
- Strawberry Shortcake
- Carrot Cake
- Pumpkin Pie
- Cinnamon Rolls
- Blackberry Pie
- Cherry Pie
- Coconut Cream Pie
- S'mores Bars
- Raspberry Tart
- Sugar Cookies
- Peach Cobbler
- Mississippi Mud Pie
- Snickerdoodles
- Oatmeal Raisin Cookies
- Apple Crisp
- Chocolate Brownies
- Pumpkin Bread
- Lemon Meringue Pie
- Peanut Butter Brownies
- Coffee Cake
- Chocolate Cake
- Cranberry Orange Scones
- Pineapple Upside-Down Cake
- Biscuits and Gravy

- Strawberry Rhubarb Pie
- Almond Biscotti
- Eclairs
- Baklava
- Rugelach
- Texas Sheet Cake
- Whoopie Pies
- Danish Pastries
- Lemon Pound Cake
- Fig Newtons
- Apple Turnovers
- Chocolate Soufflé
- Bourbon Pecan Tarts
- Cherry Bakewell Tart
- Buttermilk Pie

Classic Apple Pie

Ingredients:

For the crust:

- 2 1/2 cups all-purpose flour
- 1 teaspoon salt
- 1 teaspoon granulated sugar
- 1 cup unsalted butter, cold and cut into cubes
- 1/4 to 1/2 cup ice water

For the filling:

- 6 cups thinly sliced, peeled apples (such as Granny Smith or Honeycrisp)
- 3/4 cup granulated sugar
- 2 tablespoons all-purpose flour
- 1 teaspoon ground cinnamon
- 1/4 teaspoon ground nutmeg
- 1 tablespoon lemon juice
- 2 tablespoons unsalted butter, cut into small pieces

Instructions:

1. Prepare the Crust:
    - In a large mixing bowl, combine flour, salt, and sugar.
    - Add the cold butter cubes and use a pastry cutter or your fingers to work the butter into the flour mixture until it resembles coarse crumbs.
    - Gradually add ice water, 1 tablespoon at a time, mixing gently until the dough starts to come together. Be careful not to overwork the dough.
    - Divide the dough into two equal parts, shape each into a disk, wrap them in plastic wrap, and refrigerate for at least 1 hour.
2. Make the Filling:
    - In a large bowl, toss the sliced apples with lemon juice to prevent browning.
    - In a separate bowl, mix together sugar, flour, cinnamon, and nutmeg.
    - Add the dry mixture to the apples and toss until evenly coated.
3. Assemble the Pie:
    - Preheat your oven to 425°F (220°C).

- Roll out one disk of dough on a floured surface into a circle large enough to line a 9-inch pie dish. Transfer the dough to the pie dish and gently press it into the bottom and sides.
- Pour the apple filling into the pie crust, spreading it evenly.
- Dot the filling with small pieces of butter.
- Roll out the second disk of dough and place it over the filling. Trim any excess dough and crimp the edges to seal. Cut a few slits in the top crust to allow steam to escape.

4. Bake the Pie:
    - Place the pie on a baking sheet to catch any drips.
    - Bake for 45 to 55 minutes, or until the crust is golden brown and the filling is bubbly.
    - If the crust begins to brown too quickly, cover the edges with foil or a pie shield.
    - Allow the pie to cool for at least 1 hour before slicing and serving.

Enjoy your classic American apple pie, either on its own or with a scoop of vanilla ice cream!

Blueberry Cobbler

Ingredients:

For the filling:

- 6 cups fresh or frozen blueberries
- 1/2 cup granulated sugar
- 2 tablespoons cornstarch
- 1 tablespoon freshly squeezed lemon juice
- Zest of 1 lemon
- 1 teaspoon vanilla extract

For the topping:

- 1 1/2 cups all-purpose flour
- 1/2 cup granulated sugar
- 1 1/2 teaspoons baking powder
- 1/2 teaspoon salt
- 1/2 cup (1 stick) unsalted butter, cold and cut into small cubes
- 1/4 cup boiling water
- 2 tablespoons granulated sugar (for sprinkling)

Instructions:

1. Preheat the Oven:
    - Preheat your oven to 375°F (190°C). Lightly grease a 9x13-inch baking dish or similar size.
2. Prepare the Filling:
    - In a large bowl, gently toss together the blueberries, sugar, cornstarch, lemon juice, lemon zest, and vanilla extract until the blueberries are evenly coated. Transfer the mixture to the prepared baking dish and spread it out evenly.
3. Make the Topping:
    - In a separate mixing bowl, combine the flour, sugar, baking powder, and salt.
    - Add the cold cubed butter to the flour mixture. Using a pastry cutter or your fingers, work the butter into the flour until the mixture resembles coarse crumbs.

        - Pour the boiling water over the flour-butter mixture and stir until just combined. The dough will be thick and slightly sticky.
    4. Assemble and Bake:
        - Drop spoonfuls of the topping mixture over the blueberry filling, covering it as evenly as possible.
        - Sprinkle the top of the cobbler with the remaining 2 tablespoons of granulated sugar.
        - Place the baking dish on a baking sheet to catch any potential drips and bake in the preheated oven for 40 to 45 minutes, or until the topping is golden brown and the filling is bubbling.
        - Allow the cobbler to cool for about 15 minutes before serving.

Serve warm, either plain or topped with a scoop of vanilla ice cream or a dollop of whipped cream. Enjoy the deliciousness of homemade blueberry cobbler!

Chocolate Chip Cookies

Ingredients:

- 1 cup (2 sticks) unsalted butter, softened
- 3/4 cup granulated sugar
- 3/4 cup packed brown sugar
- 2 large eggs
- 1 teaspoon vanilla extract
- 2 1/4 cups all-purpose flour
- 1 teaspoon baking soda
- 1/2 teaspoon salt
- 2 cups semisweet chocolate chips

Instructions:

1. Preheat the Oven:
    - Preheat your oven to 375°F (190°C). Line baking sheets with parchment paper or silicone baking mats.
2. Cream Butter and Sugars:
    - In a large mixing bowl, cream together the softened butter, granulated sugar, and brown sugar until light and fluffy.
3. Add Eggs and Vanilla:
    - Beat in the eggs, one at a time, followed by the vanilla extract. Mix until well combined.
4. Combine Dry Ingredients:
    - In a separate bowl, whisk together the all-purpose flour, baking soda, and salt.
5. Combine Wet and Dry Ingredients:
    - Gradually add the dry ingredients to the wet ingredients, mixing until just combined. Be careful not to overmix.
    - Fold in the chocolate chips until evenly distributed throughout the dough.
6. Scoop and Bake:
    - Using a cookie scoop or spoon, drop rounded tablespoons of dough onto the prepared baking sheets, spacing them about 2 inches apart.
    - Bake in the preheated oven for 9 to 11 minutes, or until the cookies are golden brown around the edges and set in the center.
    - If baking multiple sheets at once, rotate the sheets halfway through baking for even browning.

7. Cool and Enjoy:
    - Allow the cookies to cool on the baking sheets for a few minutes before transferring them to a wire rack to cool completely.
    - Enjoy your freshly baked chocolate chip cookies with a glass of milk or your favorite hot beverage!

This recipe yields about 3 dozen delicious chocolate chip cookies, perfect for sharing with friends and family or enjoying all to yourself.

New York Cheesecake

Ingredients:

For the crust:

- 2 cups graham cracker crumbs
- 1/4 cup granulated sugar
- 1/2 cup (1 stick) unsalted butter, melted

For the filling:

- 4 (8-ounce) packages cream cheese, softened
- 1 1/4 cups granulated sugar
- 4 large eggs
- 2 teaspoons vanilla extract
- 1 cup sour cream
- 1/4 cup all-purpose flour
- 1/4 cup heavy cream

Instructions:

1. Preheat the Oven:
    - Preheat your oven to 325°F (160°C). Grease a 9-inch springform pan with butter or non-stick cooking spray.
2. Make the Crust:
    - In a medium bowl, combine the graham cracker crumbs, sugar, and melted butter until the mixture resembles wet sand.
    - Press the mixture evenly into the bottom of the prepared springform pan, using the bottom of a glass or measuring cup to compact it.
    - Bake the crust in the preheated oven for 10 minutes. Remove from the oven and set aside to cool while you prepare the filling.
3. Prepare the Filling:
    - In a large mixing bowl, beat the cream cheese and granulated sugar together until smooth and creamy.
    - Add the eggs one at a time, beating well after each addition.

- Mix in the vanilla extract, sour cream, flour, and heavy cream until smooth and well combined. Scrape down the sides of the bowl as needed to ensure thorough mixing.
4. Assemble and Bake:
    - Pour the filling over the cooled crust in the springform pan, spreading it out evenly.
    - Tap the pan gently on the counter a few times to release any air bubbles.
    - Place the cheesecake in the preheated oven and bake for 55 to 65 minutes, or until the edges are set and the center is slightly wobbly.
    - Turn off the oven and leave the cheesecake inside with the door slightly ajar for 1 hour to cool gradually.
5. Chill and Serve:
    - Remove the cheesecake from the oven and run a knife around the edge of the pan to loosen the cheesecake from the sides.
    - Refrigerate the cheesecake for at least 4 hours, preferably overnight, to chill and set completely.
    - Before serving, release the sides of the springform pan and transfer the cheesecake to a serving plate.
    - Slice and serve your New York cheesecake plain or with your favorite toppings, such as fresh berries, fruit compote, or whipped cream.

Enjoy the creamy indulgence of this classic New York cheesecake with its buttery graham cracker crust!

Lemon Bars

Ingredients:

For the crust:

- 1 cup all-purpose flour
- 1/2 cup unsalted butter, softened
- 1/4 cup powdered sugar

For the filling:

- 4 large eggs
- 1 1/2 cups granulated sugar
- 1/3 cup freshly squeezed lemon juice (about 2-3 lemons)
- Zest of 1 lemon
- 1/4 cup all-purpose flour
- 1/2 teaspoon baking powder
- Powdered sugar, for dusting

Instructions:

1. Preheat the Oven:
    - Preheat your oven to 350°F (175°C). Grease or line a 9x13-inch baking pan with parchment paper.
2. Make the Crust:
    - In a mixing bowl, cream together the softened butter and powdered sugar until light and fluffy.
    - Gradually add the flour and mix until a dough forms.
    - Press the dough evenly into the bottom of the prepared baking pan.
    - Bake the crust in the preheated oven for 15-20 minutes, or until lightly golden brown.
3. Prepare the Filling:
    - In another mixing bowl, whisk together the eggs, granulated sugar, lemon juice, and lemon zest until well combined.
    - In a separate bowl, sift together the flour and baking powder. Gradually add the flour mixture to the egg mixture, whisking until smooth.

4. Bake the Lemon Bars:
   - Pour the filling over the baked crust, spreading it out evenly.
   - Return the pan to the oven and bake for an additional 20-25 minutes, or until the filling is set and the edges are lightly golden brown.
   - Remove from the oven and let the lemon bars cool completely in the pan.
5. Chill and Serve:
   - Once cooled, refrigerate the lemon bars for at least 1 hour to firm up before slicing.
   - Dust the top of the lemon bars with powdered sugar.
   - Use a sharp knife to cut the lemon bars into squares.
   - Serve chilled and enjoy the tangy sweetness of these homemade lemon bars!

These lemon bars are perfect for any occasion, whether it's a summer picnic, potluck, or just a sweet treat for yourself.

Red Velvet Cupcakes

Ingredients:

For the cupcakes:

- 1 1/4 cups all-purpose flour
- 1/4 cup unsweetened cocoa powder
- 1/2 teaspoon baking soda
- 1/4 teaspoon salt
- 1/2 cup unsalted butter, softened
- 1 cup granulated sugar
- 2 large eggs
- 1 teaspoon vanilla extract
- 1/2 cup buttermilk
- 1 tablespoon red food coloring
- 1 teaspoon distilled white vinegar
- 1 teaspoon baking powder

For the cream cheese frosting:

- 8 ounces cream cheese, softened
- 1/2 cup unsalted butter, softened
- 3-4 cups powdered sugar
- 1 teaspoon vanilla extract

Instructions:

1. Preheat the Oven:
    - Preheat your oven to 350°F (175°C). Line a muffin tin with paper liners.
2. Make the Cupcake Batter:
    - In a medium bowl, sift together the flour, cocoa powder, baking soda, and salt. Set aside.
    - In a large mixing bowl, cream together the softened butter and granulated sugar until light and fluffy.
    - Add the eggs one at a time, beating well after each addition. Mix in the vanilla extract.

- In a small bowl, whisk together the buttermilk and red food coloring until well combined.
- Gradually add the dry ingredients to the creamed mixture, alternating with the buttermilk mixture, beginning and ending with the dry ingredients. Mix until just combined.
- In a small bowl, mix together the vinegar and baking powder. Quickly fold this mixture into the batter until well combined.
- Divide the batter evenly among the prepared muffin cups, filling each about two-thirds full.

3. Bake the Cupcakes:
    - Bake in the preheated oven for 18-20 minutes, or until a toothpick inserted into the center of a cupcake comes out clean.
    - Remove the cupcakes from the oven and transfer them to a wire rack to cool completely before frosting.
4. Make the Cream Cheese Frosting:
    - In a large mixing bowl, beat together the softened cream cheese and butter until smooth and creamy.
    - Gradually add the powdered sugar, one cup at a time, until the frosting reaches your desired sweetness and consistency.
    - Mix in the vanilla extract until well combined.
5. Frost the Cupcakes:
    - Once the cupcakes have cooled completely, frost them generously with the cream cheese frosting using a spatula or piping bag.
    - Optionally, decorate the frosted cupcakes with sprinkles, chocolate shavings, or a dusting of cocoa powder.
    - Serve and enjoy these delicious red velvet cupcakes!

These cupcakes are perfect for birthdays, holidays, or any special occasion where you want to impress with a classic dessert!

Pecan Pie

Ingredients:

For the crust:

- 1 1/4 cups all-purpose flour
- 1/2 teaspoon salt
- 1/2 cup (1 stick) unsalted butter, chilled and cut into small cubes
- 2-4 tablespoons ice water

For the filling:

- 1 cup granulated sugar
- 1 cup light corn syrup
- 3 large eggs
- 1 teaspoon vanilla extract
- 2 tablespoons unsalted butter, melted
- 1 1/2 cups pecan halves

Instructions:

1. Prepare the Crust:
    - In a large mixing bowl, whisk together the flour and salt.
    - Add the chilled butter cubes to the flour mixture. Use a pastry cutter or your fingers to work the butter into the flour until the mixture resembles coarse crumbs.
    - Gradually add the ice water, 1 tablespoon at a time, mixing gently with a fork until the dough comes together and forms a ball. Be careful not to overwork the dough.
    - Shape the dough into a disk, wrap it in plastic wrap, and refrigerate for at least 30 minutes.
2. Roll out the Crust:
    - Preheat your oven to 375°F (190°C).
    - On a lightly floured surface, roll out the chilled dough into a circle large enough to line a 9-inch pie dish. Carefully transfer the dough to the pie dish, pressing it gently into the bottom and up the sides. Trim any excess dough and crimp the edges as desired.
3. Prepare the Filling:

- In a medium mixing bowl, whisk together the granulated sugar, corn syrup, eggs, vanilla extract, and melted butter until well combined.
- Stir in the pecan halves until evenly coated.

4. Assemble and Bake:
   - Pour the pecan filling into the prepared pie crust, spreading it out evenly.
   - If desired, arrange a few extra pecan halves on top for decoration.
   - Place the pie on a baking sheet to catch any potential spills and bake in the preheated oven for 40 to 50 minutes, or until the filling is set and the crust is golden brown.
   - If the crust begins to brown too quickly, cover the edges with foil or a pie crust shield halfway through baking.

5. Cool and Serve:
   - Allow the pecan pie to cool completely on a wire rack before slicing and serving.
   - Serve slices of pecan pie on their own or with a dollop of whipped cream or a scoop of vanilla ice cream for an extra treat.

Enjoy the rich, nutty sweetness of this classic pecan pie with its buttery, flaky crust!

Key Lime Pie

Ingredients:

For the crust:

- 1 1/2 cups graham cracker crumbs
- 1/4 cup granulated sugar
- 6 tablespoons unsalted butter, melted

For the filling:

- 4 large egg yolks
- 14 ounces sweetened condensed milk
- 1/2 cup freshly squeezed key lime juice (about 20-25 key limes)
- 1 tablespoon key lime zest

For the topping (optional):

- 1 cup heavy whipping cream
- 2 tablespoons powdered sugar
- Lime slices or zest for garnish

Instructions:

1. Preheat the Oven:
    - Preheat your oven to 350°F (175°C). Grease a 9-inch pie dish with butter or non-stick cooking spray.
2. Make the Crust:
    - In a medium mixing bowl, combine the graham cracker crumbs, granulated sugar, and melted butter until evenly moistened.
    - Press the mixture firmly and evenly into the bottom and up the sides of the prepared pie dish.
    - Bake the crust in the preheated oven for 10 minutes. Remove from the oven and let it cool while you prepare the filling.
3. Prepare the Filling:

- In a large mixing bowl, whisk together the egg yolks and sweetened condensed milk until smooth and creamy.
- Gradually whisk in the key lime juice and zest until well combined.
4. Bake the Pie:
    - Pour the filling into the cooled graham cracker crust, spreading it out evenly.
    - Bake the pie in the preheated oven for 15-20 minutes, or until the filling is set but still slightly jiggly in the center.
    - Remove the pie from the oven and let it cool to room temperature. Once cooled, refrigerate the pie for at least 2 hours, or until well chilled and set.
5. Optional Topping:
    - In a chilled mixing bowl, whip the heavy cream and powdered sugar together until stiff peaks form.
    - Spread or pipe the whipped cream over the chilled pie.
    - Garnish with lime slices or zest, if desired.
6. Serve and Enjoy:
    - Slice the chilled Key Lime Pie and serve it cold.
    - Store any leftovers in the refrigerator.

Enjoy the tangy and refreshing flavor of this classic Key Lime Pie, perfect for any occasion, especially during warm weather!

Boston Cream Pie

Ingredients:

For the cake:

- 1 cup all-purpose flour
- 1 teaspoon baking powder
- 1/4 teaspoon salt
- 4 large eggs, at room temperature
- 1 cup granulated sugar
- 1/4 cup unsalted butter, melted
- 1/2 cup whole milk
- 1 teaspoon vanilla extract

For the custard filling:

- 2 cups whole milk
- 1/2 cup granulated sugar
- 4 large egg yolks
- 1/4 cup cornstarch
- 1 teaspoon vanilla extract

For the chocolate ganache:

- 4 ounces semisweet chocolate, chopped
- 1/2 cup heavy cream

Instructions:

1. Preheat the Oven:
    - Preheat your oven to 350°F (175°C). Grease and flour two 9-inch round cake pans.
2. Make the Cake:
    - In a medium bowl, sift together the flour, baking powder, and salt. Set aside.
    - In a large mixing bowl, beat the eggs and granulated sugar together with an electric mixer on high speed until thick and pale yellow, about 5 minutes.

- Gradually add the melted butter, milk, and vanilla extract to the egg mixture, mixing until well combined.
- Gently fold in the dry ingredients until just incorporated. Be careful not to overmix.
- Divide the batter evenly between the prepared cake pans and smooth the tops with a spatula.
- Bake in the preheated oven for 20-25 minutes, or until a toothpick inserted into the center of the cakes comes out clean.
- Remove the cakes from the oven and let them cool in the pans for 10 minutes before transferring them to wire racks to cool completely.

3. Make the Custard Filling:
   - In a medium saucepan, heat the milk over medium heat until it just begins to simmer. Remove from heat.
   - In a separate mixing bowl, whisk together the granulated sugar, egg yolks, and cornstarch until smooth and pale yellow.
   - Slowly pour the hot milk into the egg mixture, whisking constantly to temper the eggs.
   - Return the mixture to the saucepan and cook over medium heat, stirring constantly, until it thickens and comes to a boil.
   - Remove from heat and stir in the vanilla extract.
   - Transfer the custard to a clean bowl and cover it with plastic wrap, pressing the wrap directly onto the surface of the custard to prevent a skin from forming. Refrigerate until completely chilled.

4. Assemble the Pie:
   - Once the cakes and custard are completely cooled, place one cake layer on a serving plate or cake stand.
   - Spread the chilled custard evenly over the top of the cake layer.
   - Place the second cake layer on top of the custard, gently pressing down to adhere.
   - Refrigerate the assembled cake while you prepare the chocolate ganache.

5. Make the Chocolate Ganache:
   - Place the chopped chocolate in a heatproof bowl.
   - In a small saucepan, heat the heavy cream over medium heat until it just begins to simmer.
   - Pour the hot cream over the chopped chocolate and let it sit for 1-2 minutes.
   - Stir the chocolate and cream together until smooth and glossy.

6. Finish the Pie:

- Pour the chocolate ganache over the top of the assembled cake, allowing it to drip down the sides.
- Refrigerate the Boston Cream Pie for at least 1 hour to allow the ganache to set before serving.

7. Serve and Enjoy:
    - Slice the chilled Boston Cream Pie and serve it cold.
    - Store any leftovers in the refrigerator.

Enjoy the decadent combination of moist cake, creamy custard, and rich chocolate ganache in this classic Boston Cream Pie!

Banana Bread

Ingredients:

- 2 to 3 ripe bananas, mashed (about 1 cup)
- 1/3 cup unsalted butter, melted
- 3/4 cup granulated sugar
- 1 large egg, beaten
- 1 teaspoon vanilla extract
- 1 1/2 cups all-purpose flour
- 1 teaspoon baking soda
- 1/4 teaspoon salt
- 1/2 teaspoon ground cinnamon (optional)
- 1/2 cup chopped nuts (such as walnuts or pecans) or chocolate chips (optional)

Instructions:

1. Preheat the Oven:
    - Preheat your oven to 350°F (175°C). Grease a 9x5-inch loaf pan or line it with parchment paper.
2. Prepare the Batter:
    - In a large mixing bowl, mash the ripe bananas with a fork until smooth.
    - Stir in the melted butter until well combined.
    - Add the granulated sugar, beaten egg, and vanilla extract to the banana mixture, and mix until smooth.
3. Combine Dry Ingredients:
    - In a separate bowl, whisk together the all-purpose flour, baking soda, salt, and ground cinnamon (if using).
4. Mix Wet and Dry Ingredients:
    - Gradually add the dry ingredients to the wet ingredients, stirring until just combined. Be careful not to overmix.
    - If using, fold in the chopped nuts or chocolate chips until evenly distributed throughout the batter.
5. Bake the Banana Bread:
    - Pour the batter into the prepared loaf pan, spreading it out evenly.
    - Bake in the preheated oven for 50 to 60 minutes, or until a toothpick inserted into the center of the loaf comes out clean.
    - If the top of the bread starts to brown too quickly, you can loosely cover it with aluminum foil halfway through baking to prevent over-browning.

6. Cool and Serve:
   - Once baked, remove the banana bread from the oven and let it cool in the loaf pan for 10 minutes.
   - Transfer the bread to a wire rack to cool completely before slicing and serving.
7. Enjoy:
   - Slice the cooled banana bread and serve it as a delicious snack or breakfast treat.
   - Store any leftover banana bread in an airtight container at room temperature for up to 3 days, or freeze for longer storage.

Enjoy the wonderful aroma and comforting taste of homemade banana bread!

Peanut Butter Cookies

Ingredients:

- 1/2 cup (1 stick) unsalted butter, softened
- 1/2 cup creamy peanut butter
- 1/2 cup granulated sugar
- 1/2 cup packed brown sugar
- 1 large egg
- 1 teaspoon vanilla extract
- 1 1/4 cups all-purpose flour
- 1/2 teaspoon baking powder
- 1/2 teaspoon baking soda
- 1/4 teaspoon salt
- Additional granulated sugar for rolling (optional)

Instructions:

1. Preheat the Oven:
   - Preheat your oven to 350°F (175°C). Line baking sheets with parchment paper or silicone baking mats.
2. Cream Butter and Sugars:
   - In a large mixing bowl, cream together the softened butter, peanut butter, granulated sugar, and brown sugar until smooth and creamy.
3. Add Egg and Vanilla:
   - Beat in the egg and vanilla extract until well combined.
4. Combine Dry Ingredients:
   - In a separate bowl, whisk together the flour, baking powder, baking soda, and salt.
5. Mix Wet and Dry Ingredients:
   - Gradually add the dry ingredients to the wet ingredients, mixing until just combined. Be careful not to overmix.
6. Form Cookie Dough Balls:
   - Roll the dough into 1-inch balls and place them on the prepared baking sheets, spacing them about 2 inches apart.
   - If desired, roll the dough balls in additional granulated sugar for a slightly crunchy exterior.
7. Bake the Cookies:

- Using a fork, gently press down on each dough ball to create a crisscross pattern on top.
- Bake in the preheated oven for 10 to 12 minutes, or until the cookies are lightly golden brown around the edges.
- Remove the cookies from the oven and let them cool on the baking sheets for a few minutes before transferring them to a wire rack to cool completely.

8. Enjoy:
    - Once cooled, enjoy your homemade peanut butter cookies with a glass of milk or your favorite beverage!

These peanut butter cookies are sure to be a hit with peanut butter lovers of all ages. They're perfect for sharing with friends and family or enjoying as a special treat just for yourself!

Strawberry Shortcake

Ingredients:

For the shortcakes:

- 2 cups all-purpose flour
- 1/4 cup granulated sugar
- 1 tablespoon baking powder
- 1/2 teaspoon salt
- 1/2 cup (1 stick) unsalted butter, cold and cut into small pieces
- 3/4 cup milk
- 1 teaspoon vanilla extract

For the strawberries:

- 1 pound fresh strawberries, hulled and sliced
- 2-3 tablespoons granulated sugar (adjust to taste)
- Whipped cream, for serving

Instructions:

1. Preheat the Oven:
   - Preheat your oven to 425°F (220°C). Line a baking sheet with parchment paper or a silicone baking mat.
2. Prepare the Shortcakes:
   - In a large mixing bowl, whisk together the flour, sugar, baking powder, and salt.
   - Add the cold butter pieces to the flour mixture. Use a pastry cutter or your fingers to work the butter into the flour until the mixture resembles coarse crumbs.
   - In a separate bowl, mix together the milk and vanilla extract.
   - Gradually add the milk mixture to the flour mixture, stirring until just combined. Be careful not to overmix.
   - Turn the dough out onto a lightly floured surface and gently knead it a few times until it comes together.
   - Pat the dough into a circle about 3/4 to 1 inch thick.

- Use a round biscuit cutter or glass to cut out circles of dough. Place the dough circles onto the prepared baking sheet, spacing them about 2 inches apart.
3. Bake the Shortcakes:
    - Bake in the preheated oven for 12 to 15 minutes, or until the shortcakes are lightly golden brown.
    - Remove from the oven and let them cool on the baking sheet for a few minutes before transferring them to a wire rack to cool completely.
4. Prepare the Strawberries:
    - In a mixing bowl, combine the sliced strawberries with the granulated sugar. Toss gently to coat the strawberries in sugar. Let them sit for about 15 minutes to macerate and release their juices.
5. Assemble the Strawberry Shortcakes:
    - To serve, slice the cooled shortcakes in half horizontally.
    - Place a generous spoonful of macerated strawberries on the bottom half of each shortcake.
    - Top with a dollop of whipped cream.
    - Place the other half of the shortcake on top.
    - Optionally, garnish with additional whipped cream and whole strawberries.
6. Enjoy:
    - Serve the strawberry shortcakes immediately and enjoy the sweet, fruity goodness!

These strawberry shortcakes are perfect for spring and summer gatherings, picnics, or as a special dessert any time of year.

Carrot Cake

Ingredients:

For the cake:

- 2 cups all-purpose flour
- 2 teaspoons baking powder
- 1 1/2 teaspoons baking soda
- 1/2 teaspoon salt
- 2 teaspoons ground cinnamon
- 1/2 teaspoon ground nutmeg
- 1/2 teaspoon ground ginger
- 1 cup granulated sugar
- 1 cup packed brown sugar
- 1 cup vegetable oil
- 4 large eggs
- 2 teaspoons vanilla extract
- 3 cups grated carrots (about 3-4 medium carrots)
- 1 cup crushed pineapple, drained
- 1 cup chopped walnuts or pecans (optional)

For the cream cheese frosting:

- 8 ounces cream cheese, softened
- 1/2 cup unsalted butter, softened
- 4 cups powdered sugar
- 1 teaspoon vanilla extract

Instructions:

1. Preheat the Oven:
    - Preheat your oven to 350°F (175°C). Grease and flour two 9-inch round cake pans or line them with parchment paper.
2. Prepare the Cake Batter:
    - In a large mixing bowl, sift together the flour, baking powder, baking soda, salt, cinnamon, nutmeg, and ginger.

- In another mixing bowl, whisk together the granulated sugar, brown sugar, vegetable oil, eggs, and vanilla extract until well combined.
- Gradually add the wet ingredients to the dry ingredients, mixing until just combined.
- Fold in the grated carrots, crushed pineapple, and chopped nuts (if using) until evenly distributed throughout the batter.

3. Bake the Cake:
   - Divide the batter evenly between the prepared cake pans, spreading it out evenly.
   - Bake in the preheated oven for 30 to 35 minutes, or until a toothpick inserted into the center of the cakes comes out clean.
   - Remove the cakes from the oven and let them cool in the pans for 10 minutes before transferring them to wire racks to cool completely.

4. Make the Cream Cheese Frosting:
   - In a large mixing bowl, beat together the softened cream cheese and butter until smooth and creamy.
   - Gradually add the powdered sugar, one cup at a time, beating well after each addition, until the frosting is smooth and spreadable.
   - Mix in the vanilla extract until well combined.

5. Assemble the Cake:
   - Once the cakes are completely cooled, place one cake layer on a serving plate or cake stand.
   - Spread a layer of cream cheese frosting over the top of the cake layer.
   - Place the second cake layer on top and frost the top and sides of the cake with the remaining cream cheese frosting.

6. Decorate (optional):
   - Optionally, garnish the cake with additional chopped nuts or shredded carrots for decoration.

7. Chill and Serve:
   - Chill the carrot cake in the refrigerator for at least 30 minutes before serving to allow the frosting to set.
   - Slice and serve the chilled carrot cake, and enjoy!

This carrot cake is perfect for celebrations, special occasions, or as a comforting treat any time of year. The combination of moist cake and creamy frosting is sure to be a hit!

Pumpkin Pie

Ingredients:

For the pie crust:

- 1 1/4 cups all-purpose flour
- 1/2 teaspoon salt
- 1/2 teaspoon granulated sugar
- 1/2 cup (1 stick) cold unsalted butter, cut into small pieces
- 3 to 4 tablespoons ice water

For the filling:

- 1 (15-ounce) can pumpkin puree (about 1 3/4 cups)
- 3/4 cup packed light brown sugar
- 1 teaspoon ground cinnamon
- 1/2 teaspoon ground ginger
- 1/4 teaspoon ground nutmeg
- 1/4 teaspoon ground cloves
- 1/2 teaspoon salt
- 2 large eggs
- 1 cup evaporated milk or heavy cream

Instructions:

1. Prepare the Pie Crust:
    - In a large mixing bowl, whisk together the flour, salt, and granulated sugar.
    - Add the cold butter pieces to the flour mixture. Use a pastry cutter or your fingers to work the butter into the flour until the mixture resembles coarse crumbs.
    - Gradually add the ice water, 1 tablespoon at a time, mixing gently with a fork until the dough comes together and forms a ball. Be careful not to overwork the dough.
    - Shape the dough into a disk, wrap it in plastic wrap, and refrigerate for at least 30 minutes.
2. Preheat the Oven:
    - Preheat your oven to 425°F (220°C). Place a baking sheet in the oven to preheat as well.

3. Roll out the Pie Crust:
   - On a lightly floured surface, roll out the chilled dough into a circle large enough to line a 9-inch pie dish. Carefully transfer the dough to the pie dish, gently pressing it into the bottom and up the sides. Trim any excess dough and crimp the edges as desired.
4. Prepare the Pumpkin Filling:
   - In a large mixing bowl, whisk together the pumpkin puree, brown sugar, cinnamon, ginger, nutmeg, cloves, and salt until well combined.
   - Add the eggs and evaporated milk (or heavy cream) to the pumpkin mixture, and whisk until smooth and creamy.
5. Fill and Bake the Pie:
   - Pour the pumpkin filling into the prepared pie crust, spreading it out evenly.
   - Place the pie on the preheated baking sheet in the oven and bake for 15 minutes.
   - Reduce the oven temperature to 350°F (175°C) and continue baking for 45 to 50 minutes, or until the filling is set and a knife inserted into the center comes out clean.
6. Cool and Serve:
   - Remove the pie from the oven and let it cool completely on a wire rack before serving.
   - Serve slices of pumpkin pie with whipped cream or vanilla ice cream, if desired.

Enjoy the rich, creamy, and spiced flavor of this classic pumpkin pie, a perfect addition to your holiday dessert table!

Cinnamon Rolls

Ingredients:

For the dough:

- 1 cup warm milk (about 110°F)
- 2 1/4 teaspoons active dry yeast (1 packet)
- 1/2 cup granulated sugar
- 1/3 cup unsalted butter, melted
- 2 large eggs, room temperature
- 4 1/2 cups all-purpose flour
- 1 teaspoon salt

For the cinnamon filling:

- 1/3 cup unsalted butter, softened
- 1 cup packed brown sugar
- 2 tablespoons ground cinnamon

For the icing:

- 4 ounces cream cheese, softened
- 1/4 cup unsalted butter, softened
- 1 1/2 cups powdered sugar
- 1/2 teaspoon vanilla extract

Instructions:

1. Activate the Yeast:
    - In a large mixing bowl, combine the warm milk and active dry yeast. Let it sit for about 5 minutes until the yeast is foamy.
2. Make the Dough:
    - To the bowl with the activated yeast, add the granulated sugar, melted butter, eggs, flour, and salt.
    - Mix the ingredients together until a soft dough forms.
    - Knead the dough on a lightly floured surface for about 5-7 minutes until it becomes smooth and elastic.
3. First Rise:

- Place the dough in a greased bowl, cover it with a clean kitchen towel, and let it rise in a warm place for about 1 hour, or until it doubles in size.
4. Make the Cinnamon Filling:
    - In a small bowl, mix together the softened butter, brown sugar, and ground cinnamon until well combined.
5. Roll out the Dough:
    - After the dough has risen, punch it down and roll it out into a large rectangle on a floured surface, about 16x20 inches.
6. Fill and Roll:
    - Spread the cinnamon filling evenly over the rolled-out dough, leaving about a 1-inch border around the edges.
    - Starting from one long side, tightly roll up the dough into a log.
    - Pinch the seam to seal.
7. Cut into Rolls:
    - Using a sharp knife or unflavored dental floss, cut the log into 12 equal-sized rolls.
8. Second Rise:
    - Place the rolls in a greased 9x13-inch baking pan, leaving a little space between each roll.
    - Cover the pan with a kitchen towel and let the rolls rise for another 30-45 minutes, until they are puffy.
9. Bake the Rolls:
    - Preheat your oven to 375°F (190°C).
    - Once the rolls have risen, bake them in the preheated oven for 20-25 minutes, or until they are golden brown on top and cooked through.
10. Make the Icing:
    - While the rolls are baking, prepare the icing. In a mixing bowl, beat together the softened cream cheese, softened butter, powdered sugar, and vanilla extract until smooth and creamy.
11. Ice the Rolls:
    - Once the rolls are out of the oven, let them cool for a few minutes, then spread the icing over the warm rolls.
12. Serve and Enjoy:
    - Serve the cinnamon rolls warm and enjoy the irresistible combination of soft dough, sweet cinnamon filling, and creamy icing!

These homemade cinnamon rolls are perfect for breakfast, brunch, or as a special treat any time of day. Enjoy!

Blackberry Pie

Ingredients:

For the crust:

- 2 1/2 cups all-purpose flour
- 1 teaspoon salt
- 1 tablespoon granulated sugar
- 1 cup (2 sticks) cold unsalted butter, cut into small pieces
- 6-8 tablespoons ice water

For the filling:

- 6 cups fresh blackberries, rinsed and drained
- 3/4 cup granulated sugar (adjust based on the sweetness of the berries)
- 1/4 cup cornstarch
- 1 tablespoon lemon juice
- 1 teaspoon lemon zest
- 1/2 teaspoon ground cinnamon (optional)
- 1/4 teaspoon salt
- 1 tablespoon unsalted butter, cut into small pieces

For egg wash (optional):

- 1 large egg
- 1 tablespoon water

Instructions:

1. Prepare the Crust:
    - In a large mixing bowl, whisk together the flour, salt, and granulated sugar.
    - Add the cold butter pieces to the flour mixture. Use a pastry cutter or your fingers to work the butter into the flour until the mixture resembles coarse crumbs.
    - Gradually add the ice water, 1 tablespoon at a time, mixing gently with a fork until the dough comes together and forms a ball. Be careful not to overwork the dough.
    - Divide the dough in half, shape each half into a disk, wrap them in plastic wrap, and refrigerate for at least 1 hour.

2. Preheat the Oven:
   - Preheat your oven to 400°F (200°C). Place a baking sheet in the oven to preheat as well.
3. Make the Filling:
   - In a large mixing bowl, gently toss together the blackberries, granulated sugar, cornstarch, lemon juice, lemon zest, ground cinnamon (if using), and salt until the berries are evenly coated.
4. Roll out the Dough:
   - On a lightly floured surface, roll out one disk of chilled dough into a circle large enough to line a 9-inch pie dish. Carefully transfer the dough to the pie dish, gently pressing it into the bottom and up the sides.
   - Trim any excess dough hanging over the edges of the pie dish.
5. Fill the Pie:
   - Pour the blackberry filling into the prepared pie crust, spreading it out evenly.
   - Dot the top of the filling with small pieces of unsalted butter.
6. Roll out the Top Crust:
   - Roll out the second disk of chilled dough into a circle large enough to cover the pie.
   - Place the dough over the filling, and trim any excess dough hanging over the edges.
7. Seal and Vent the Pie:
   - Fold and crimp the edges of the bottom and top crusts together to seal the pie.
   - Cut several slits or a decorative pattern in the top crust to allow steam to escape during baking.
8. Optional Egg Wash:
   - In a small bowl, whisk together the egg and water. Brush the top crust with the egg wash for a golden finish.
9. Bake the Pie:
   - Place the pie on the preheated baking sheet in the oven and bake for 45 to 55 minutes, or until the crust is golden brown and the filling is bubbling.
10. Cool and Serve:
    - Remove the pie from the oven and let it cool on a wire rack for at least 2 hours before slicing and serving.
11. Enjoy:
    - Serve slices of blackberry pie with a scoop of vanilla ice cream or a dollop of whipped cream, if desired.

This homemade blackberry pie is bursting with sweet and tangy flavor, making it the perfect dessert for any occasion!

Cherry Pie

Ingredients:

For the crust:

- 2 1/2 cups all-purpose flour
- 1 teaspoon salt
- 1 tablespoon granulated sugar
- 1 cup (2 sticks) cold unsalted butter, cut into small pieces
- 6-8 tablespoons ice water

For the filling:

- 5 cups fresh or frozen cherries, pitted
- 3/4 cup granulated sugar (adjust based on the sweetness of the cherries)
- 1/4 cup cornstarch
- 1 tablespoon lemon juice
- 1 teaspoon vanilla extract
- 1/4 teaspoon almond extract (optional)
- 1/4 teaspoon ground cinnamon (optional)
- 1 tablespoon unsalted butter, cut into small pieces

For egg wash (optional):

- 1 large egg
- 1 tablespoon water

Instructions:

1. Prepare the Crust:
    - In a large mixing bowl, whisk together the flour, salt, and granulated sugar.
    - Add the cold butter pieces to the flour mixture. Use a pastry cutter or your fingers to work the butter into the flour until the mixture resembles coarse crumbs.

- Gradually add the ice water, 1 tablespoon at a time, mixing gently with a fork until the dough comes together and forms a ball. Be careful not to overwork the dough.
- Divide the dough in half, shape each half into a disk, wrap them in plastic wrap, and refrigerate for at least 1 hour.

2. Preheat the Oven:
    - Preheat your oven to 400°F (200°C). Place a baking sheet in the oven to preheat as well.
3. Make the Filling:
    - In a large mixing bowl, gently toss together the pitted cherries, granulated sugar, cornstarch, lemon juice, vanilla extract, almond extract (if using), and ground cinnamon (if using) until the cherries are evenly coated.
4. Roll out the Dough:
    - On a lightly floured surface, roll out one disk of chilled dough into a circle large enough to line a 9-inch pie dish. Carefully transfer the dough to the pie dish, gently pressing it into the bottom and up the sides.
    - Trim any excess dough hanging over the edges of the pie dish.
5. Fill the Pie:
    - Pour the cherry filling into the prepared pie crust, spreading it out evenly.
    - Dot the top of the filling with small pieces of unsalted butter.
6. Roll out the Top Crust:
    - Roll out the second disk of chilled dough into a circle large enough to cover the pie.
    - Place the dough over the filling, and trim any excess dough hanging over the edges.
7. Seal and Vent the Pie:
    - Fold and crimp the edges of the bottom and top crusts together to seal the pie.
    - Cut several slits or a decorative pattern in the top crust to allow steam to escape during baking.
8. Optional Egg Wash:
    - In a small bowl, whisk together the egg and water. Brush the top crust with the egg wash for a golden finish.
9. Bake the Pie:
    - Place the pie on the preheated baking sheet in the oven and bake for 45 to 55 minutes, or until the crust is golden brown and the filling is bubbling.
10. Cool and Serve:
    - Remove the pie from the oven and let it cool on a wire rack for at least 2 hours before slicing and serving.

11. Enjoy:
    - Serve slices of cherry pie with a scoop of vanilla ice cream or a dollop of whipped cream, if desired.

This homemade cherry pie is a classic dessert that's perfect for any occasion, from casual gatherings to holiday feasts!

Coconut Cream Pie

Ingredients:

For the crust:

- 1 1/4 cups all-purpose flour
- 1/2 teaspoon salt
- 1/2 teaspoon granulated sugar
- 1/2 cup (1 stick) cold unsalted butter, cut into small pieces
- 4-6 tablespoons ice water

For the filling:

- 1 (13.5-ounce) can coconut milk
- 1 cup whole milk
- 1 cup granulated sugar
- 1/3 cup cornstarch
- 1/4 teaspoon salt
- 4 large egg yolks
- 2 teaspoons vanilla extract
- 1 1/2 cups sweetened shredded coconut, divided
- 2 tablespoons unsalted butter

For the topping:

- 1 1/2 cups heavy cream
- 1/4 cup powdered sugar
- 1/2 teaspoon vanilla extract
- Toasted coconut flakes, for garnish (optional)

Instructions:

1. Prepare the Crust:
    - In a large mixing bowl, whisk together the flour, salt, and granulated sugar.

- Add the cold butter pieces to the flour mixture. Use a pastry cutter or your fingers to work the butter into the flour until the mixture resembles coarse crumbs.
- Gradually add the ice water, 1 tablespoon at a time, mixing gently with a fork until the dough comes together and forms a ball. Be careful not to overwork the dough.
- Flatten the dough into a disk, wrap it in plastic wrap, and refrigerate for at least 1 hour.

2. Preheat the Oven:
   - Preheat your oven to 375°F (190°C). Roll out the chilled dough on a lightly floured surface into a circle large enough to line a 9-inch pie dish. Carefully transfer the dough to the pie dish, gently pressing it into the bottom and up the sides. Trim any excess dough hanging over the edges.

3. Blind Bake the Crust:
   - Line the chilled pie crust with parchment paper or aluminum foil and fill it with pie weights or dried beans.
   - Bake in the preheated oven for 15 minutes. Remove the parchment paper and weights, and continue baking for another 10-15 minutes, or until the crust is golden brown. Let it cool completely.

4. Prepare the Filling:
   - In a medium saucepan, combine the coconut milk, whole milk, granulated sugar, cornstarch, and salt. Whisk until smooth.
   - Cook the mixture over medium heat, stirring constantly, until it thickens and comes to a boil.
   - In a separate bowl, whisk the egg yolks. Gradually whisk in about 1 cup of the hot milk mixture to temper the eggs.
   - Pour the tempered egg mixture back into the saucepan with the remaining hot milk mixture, whisking constantly.
   - Cook for another 2-3 minutes, stirring constantly, until the filling is thickened.
   - Remove the saucepan from the heat and stir in the vanilla extract, 1 cup of sweetened shredded coconut, and unsalted butter until well combined.

5. Assemble the Pie:
   - Pour the coconut filling into the cooled pie crust, spreading it out evenly.
   - Cover the pie with plastic wrap, pressing the wrap directly onto the surface of the filling to prevent a skin from forming.
   - Refrigerate the pie for at least 4 hours, or until chilled and set.

6. Prepare the Topping:

- In a mixing bowl, whip the heavy cream, powdered sugar, and vanilla extract until stiff peaks form.
- Spread or pipe the whipped cream over the chilled pie.
- Sprinkle the remaining 1/2 cup of sweetened shredded coconut and toasted coconut flakes over the whipped cream for garnish, if desired.

7. Serve and Enjoy:
    - Slice the chilled coconut cream pie and serve it cold.
    - Store any leftovers in the refrigerator.

Enjoy the creamy coconut filling, flaky crust, and fluffy whipped cream topping of this irresistible coconut cream pie!

S'mores Bars

Ingredients:

- 1/2 cup (1 stick) unsalted butter, melted
- 1/4 cup granulated sugar
- 1/2 cup packed brown sugar
- 1 large egg
- 1 teaspoon vanilla extract
- 1 1/3 cups all-purpose flour
- 3/4 cup graham cracker crumbs
- 1 teaspoon baking powder
- 1/4 teaspoon salt
- 2 cups mini marshmallows
- 1 cup chocolate chips or chopped chocolate bars

Instructions:

1. Preheat the Oven:
    - Preheat your oven to 350°F (175°C). Grease or line an 8x8-inch baking pan with parchment paper.
2. Prepare the Batter:
    - In a large mixing bowl, whisk together the melted butter, granulated sugar, and brown sugar until well combined.
    - Add the egg and vanilla extract, and mix until smooth.
3. Combine Dry Ingredients:
    - In a separate bowl, whisk together the all-purpose flour, graham cracker crumbs, baking powder, and salt.
4. Mix Wet and Dry Ingredients:
    - Gradually add the dry ingredients to the wet ingredients, stirring until just combined. Be careful not to overmix.
5. Assemble the Bars:
    - Press about two-thirds of the dough evenly into the bottom of the prepared baking pan to form the base layer.
    - Sprinkle the mini marshmallows evenly over the dough in the pan.
    - Sprinkle the chocolate chips or chopped chocolate evenly over the marshmallows.
6. Top with Remaining Dough:

- Take small portions of the remaining dough and flatten them between your hands to form thin discs. Place these discs over the marshmallows and chocolate, covering them as much as possible.
7. Bake the Bars:
    - Bake in the preheated oven for 20-25 minutes, or until the top is golden brown and the edges are slightly pulling away from the sides of the pan.
8. Cool and Serve:
    - Remove the pan from the oven and let the bars cool completely before slicing into squares or bars.
    - Once cooled, slice and serve the S'mores Bars.
    - Enjoy the gooey marshmallow, melted chocolate, and graham cracker goodness!

These S'mores Bars are a crowd-pleaser and perfect for picnics, parties, or simply indulging in a sweet treat at home.

Raspberry Tart

Ingredients:

- 1/2 cup (1 stick) unsalted butter, melted
- 1/4 cup granulated sugar
- 1/2 cup packed brown sugar
- 1 large egg
- 1 teaspoon vanilla extract
- 1 1/3 cups all-purpose flour
- 3/4 cup graham cracker crumbs
- 1 teaspoon baking powder
- 1/4 teaspoon salt
- 2 cups mini marshmallows
- 1 cup chocolate chips or chopped chocolate bars

Instructions:

1. Preheat the Oven:
    - Preheat your oven to 350°F (175°C). Grease or line an 8x8-inch baking pan with parchment paper.
2. Prepare the Batter:
    - In a large mixing bowl, whisk together the melted butter, granulated sugar, and brown sugar until well combined.
    - Add the egg and vanilla extract, and mix until smooth.
3. Combine Dry Ingredients:
    - In a separate bowl, whisk together the all-purpose flour, graham cracker crumbs, baking powder, and salt.
4. Mix Wet and Dry Ingredients:
    - Gradually add the dry ingredients to the wet ingredients, stirring until just combined. Be careful not to overmix.
5. Assemble the Bars:
    - Press about two-thirds of the dough evenly into the bottom of the prepared baking pan to form the base layer.
    - Sprinkle the mini marshmallows evenly over the dough in the pan.
    - Sprinkle the chocolate chips or chopped chocolate evenly over the marshmallows.
6. Top with Remaining Dough:
    - Take small portions of the remaining dough and flatten them between your hands to form thin discs. Place these discs over the marshmallows and chocolate, covering them as much as possible.
7. Bake the Bars:
    - Bake in the preheated oven for 20-25 minutes, or until the top is golden brown and the edges are slightly pulling away from the sides of the pan.

8. Cool and Serve:
    - Remove the pan from the oven and let the bars cool completely before slicing into squares or bars.
    - Once cooled, slice and serve the S'mores Bars.
    - Enjoy the gooey marshmallow, melted chocolate, and graham cracker goodness!

These S'mores Bars are a crowd-pleaser and perfect for picnics, parties, or simply indulging in a sweet treat at home.

Raspberry Tart

Here's a delightful recipe for a raspberry tart that's both visually stunning and delicious:

Ingredients:

For the crust:

- 1 1/4 cups all-purpose flour
- 1/4 cup granulated sugar
- 1/4 teaspoon salt
- 1/2 cup (1 stick) unsalted butter, cold and cut into small pieces
- 1 large egg yolk
- 1 tablespoon ice water

For the filling:

- 3 cups fresh raspberries, washed and drained
- 1/4 cup granulated sugar
- 2 tablespoons cornstarch
- 1 tablespoon lemon juice
- Zest of 1 lemon

For the glaze (optional):

- 1/4 cup seedless raspberry jam
- 1 tablespoon water

Instructions:

1. Prepare the Crust:
    - In a food processor, combine the flour, sugar, and salt. Pulse a few times to mix.
    - Add the cold butter pieces and pulse until the mixture resembles coarse crumbs.
    - Add the egg yolk and ice water, and pulse until the dough comes together.
    - Turn the dough out onto a lightly floured surface and knead briefly until smooth.
    - Shape the dough into a disk, wrap it in plastic wrap, and refrigerate for at least 30 minutes.
2. Preheat the Oven:
    - Preheat your oven to 375°F (190°C). Lightly grease a 9-inch tart pan with a removable bottom.
3. Roll out the Crust:

- On a lightly floured surface, roll out the chilled dough into a circle large enough to fit into the tart pan.
- Carefully transfer the dough to the tart pan, pressing it into the bottom and up the sides. Trim any excess dough hanging over the edges.
4. Prepare the Filling:
    - In a mixing bowl, gently toss together the fresh raspberries, granulated sugar, cornstarch, lemon juice, and lemon zest until the raspberries are evenly coated.
    - Pour the raspberry filling into the prepared tart crust, spreading it out evenly.
5. Bake the Tart:
    - Place the tart pan on a baking sheet to catch any drips, and bake in the preheated oven for 35 to 40 minutes, or until the crust is golden brown and the raspberries are bubbling.
6. Make the Glaze (optional):
    - In a small saucepan, heat the seedless raspberry jam and water over low heat until melted and smooth. Remove from heat and let it cool slightly.
7. Glaze the Tart (optional):
    - Once the tart is done baking, remove it from the oven and let it cool for about 10 minutes.
    - Brush the top of the tart with the raspberry glaze for a shiny finish.
8. Cool and Serve:
    - Allow the tart to cool completely in the pan before removing the sides of the tart pan.
    - Slice the raspberry tart and serve it at room temperature or chilled.
    - Enjoy the fresh and vibrant flavors of this delicious raspberry tart!

This raspberry tart is perfect for showcasing the natural sweetness of fresh raspberries and makes a beautiful dessert for any occasion.

Sugar Cookies

Ingredients:

- 2 3/4 cups all-purpose flour
- 1 teaspoon baking soda
- 1/2 teaspoon baking powder
- 1 cup unsalted butter, softened
- 1 1/2 cups granulated sugar
- 1 large egg
- 2 teaspoons vanilla extract
- Additional flour for rolling

Instructions:

1. Preheat the Oven:
    - Preheat your oven to 375°F (190°C). Line baking sheets with parchment paper or silicone baking mats.
2. Prepare Dry Ingredients:
    - In a medium bowl, whisk together the flour, baking soda, and baking powder. Set aside.
3. Cream Butter and Sugar:
    - In a large mixing bowl, cream together the softened butter and granulated sugar until light and fluffy, about 2-3 minutes.
4. Add Wet Ingredients:
    - Beat in the egg and vanilla extract until well combined, scraping down the sides of the bowl as needed.
5. Combine Dry and Wet Ingredients:
    - Gradually add the dry ingredients to the wet ingredients, mixing until just combined. Be careful not to overmix.
6. Chill the Dough:
    - Divide the dough in half. Flatten each half into a disk, wrap in plastic wrap, and chill in the refrigerator for at least 1 hour or until firm.
7. Roll and Cut the Cookies:
    - Once chilled, remove one disk of dough from the refrigerator and let it sit at room temperature for a few minutes to soften slightly.
    - On a lightly floured surface, roll out the dough to about 1/4 inch thick.

- Use cookie cutters to cut out shapes and transfer them to the prepared baking sheets, spacing them about 2 inches apart.
8. Bake the Cookies:
    - Bake in the preheated oven for 8-10 minutes, or until the edges are just beginning to turn golden brown.
    - Remove from the oven and let the cookies cool on the baking sheets for a few minutes before transferring them to wire racks to cool completely.
9. Decorate (optional):
    - Once the cookies are completely cooled, you can decorate them with icing, frosting, sprinkles, or any other decorations of your choice.
10. Enjoy:
    - Once decorated, let the icing set before storing the cookies in an airtight container at room temperature.

These sugar cookies are perfect for any occasion, whether you're decorating them for holidays, birthdays, or just enjoying them as a sweet treat with a cup of tea or coffee.

Peach Cobbler

Ingredients:

For the filling:

- 6 cups fresh or frozen sliced peaches (about 6-8 medium peaches)
- 1 cup granulated sugar
- 1/4 cup brown sugar
- 1/4 teaspoon ground cinnamon
- 1/8 teaspoon ground nutmeg
- 2 tablespoons lemon juice
- 2 tablespoons cornstarch

For the topping:

- 1 1/2 cups all-purpose flour
- 1/2 cup granulated sugar
- 1/4 cup brown sugar
- 1 teaspoon baking powder
- 1/2 teaspoon salt
- 1/2 cup (1 stick) unsalted butter, cold and cut into small pieces
- 1/4 cup boiling water
- 1 tablespoon granulated sugar (for topping)

Instructions:

1. Preheat the Oven:
    - Preheat your oven to 375°F (190°C). Lightly grease a 9x13-inch baking dish.
2. Prepare the Filling:
    - In a large mixing bowl, combine the sliced peaches, granulated sugar, brown sugar, ground cinnamon, ground nutmeg, lemon juice, and cornstarch. Toss until the peaches are evenly coated.
3. Transfer to Baking Dish:
    - Pour the peach mixture into the prepared baking dish and spread it out evenly.
4. Make the Topping:

- In a separate mixing bowl, whisk together the all-purpose flour, granulated sugar, brown sugar, baking powder, and salt.
- Cut in the cold butter pieces using a pastry cutter or fork until the mixture resembles coarse crumbs.
- Stir in the boiling water until just combined. The topping will be thick and somewhat lumpy.

5. Add Topping to the Cobbler:
    - Drop spoonfuls of the topping mixture over the peaches in the baking dish, covering them as much as possible.
6. Sprinkle with Sugar:
    - Sprinkle the tablespoon of granulated sugar evenly over the topping.
7. Bake the Cobbler:
    - Bake in the preheated oven for 40-45 minutes, or until the topping is golden brown and the filling is bubbly.
8. Cool and Serve:
    - Remove the peach cobbler from the oven and let it cool for a few minutes before serving.
    - Serve warm, topped with a scoop of vanilla ice cream or a dollop of whipped cream, if desired.

This homemade peach cobbler is a classic dessert that's perfect for showcasing ripe, juicy peaches. Enjoy it as a comforting treat on its own or as a delightful ending to any meal!

Mississippi Mud Pie

Ingredients:

For the crust:

- 1 1/2 cups chocolate cookie crumbs (about 20 cookies)
- 6 tablespoons unsalted butter, melted

For the filling:

- 1 cup heavy cream
- 1 cup semisweet chocolate chips
- 1/4 cup unsalted butter
- 1 teaspoon vanilla extract

For the coffee layer:

- 1 tablespoon instant coffee granules
- 1 tablespoon hot water

For the topping:

- 1 1/2 cups heavy cream
- 2 tablespoons powdered sugar
- Chocolate shavings or cocoa powder, for garnish (optional)

Instructions:

1. Prepare the Crust:
    - In a mixing bowl, combine the chocolate cookie crumbs and melted butter until well combined.
    - Press the mixture evenly into the bottom and up the sides of a 9-inch pie dish. Chill the crust in the refrigerator while you prepare the filling.
2. Make the Chocolate Filling:
    - In a saucepan, heat the heavy cream over medium heat until it just begins to simmer.

- Remove from heat and stir in the chocolate chips, unsalted butter, and vanilla extract until smooth and well combined.
- Pour the chocolate filling into the prepared crust and spread it out evenly. Place the pie dish back in the refrigerator to chill while you prepare the coffee layer.

3. Prepare the Coffee Layer:
   - In a small bowl, dissolve the instant coffee granules in hot water. Let it cool slightly.
   - Spread the coffee mixture evenly over the chilled chocolate filling.
4. Chill the Pie:
   - Return the pie to the refrigerator and chill for at least 1 hour, or until the layers are set.
5. Make the Whipped Cream Topping:
   - In a mixing bowl, beat the heavy cream and powdered sugar together until stiff peaks form.
6. Decorate and Serve:
   - Spread the whipped cream topping over the chilled pie.
   - Garnish with chocolate shavings or dust with cocoa powder, if desired.
   - Slice and serve the Mississippi Mud Pie chilled.

This decadent dessert is perfect for chocolate lovers and is sure to impress at any gathering or special occasion. Enjoy the rich layers of chocolate, coffee, and cream in every bite!

Snickerdoodles

Ingredients:

- 1 cup (2 sticks) unsalted butter, softened
- 1 1/2 cups granulated sugar
- 2 large eggs
- 2 3/4 cups all-purpose flour
- 2 teaspoons cream of tartar
- 1 teaspoon baking soda
- 1/4 teaspoon salt

For rolling:

- 1/4 cup granulated sugar
- 2 tablespoons ground cinnamon

Instructions:

1. Preheat the Oven:
    - Preheat your oven to 375°F (190°C). Line baking sheets with parchment paper or silicone baking mats.
2. Cream Butter and Sugar:
    - In a large mixing bowl, cream together the softened butter and 1 1/2 cups of granulated sugar until light and fluffy, about 2-3 minutes.
3. Add Eggs:
    - Beat in the eggs, one at a time, until well combined.
4. Combine Dry Ingredients:
    - In a separate bowl, whisk together the all-purpose flour, cream of tartar, baking soda, and salt.
5. Mix Wet and Dry Ingredients:
    - Gradually add the dry ingredients to the wet ingredients, mixing until just combined. Be careful not to overmix.
6. Prepare Rolling Mixture:
    - In a small bowl, mix together the remaining 1/4 cup of granulated sugar and ground cinnamon.
7. Form Dough Balls:
    - Roll the dough into balls, about 1 to 1 1/2 inches in diameter.
    - Roll each dough ball in the cinnamon-sugar mixture until coated evenly.

8. Place on Baking Sheets:
    - Place the coated dough balls onto the prepared baking sheets, spacing them about 2 inches apart.
9. Bake the Cookies:
    - Bake in the preheated oven for 8 to 10 minutes, or until the edges are set and the tops are just beginning to crack.
    - Remove from the oven and let the cookies cool on the baking sheets for a few minutes before transferring them to wire racks to cool completely.
10. Enjoy:
    - Once cooled, serve and enjoy these delicious homemade snickerdoodle cookies!

These snickerdoodles are soft, chewy, and have a perfect balance of sweetness and spice from the cinnamon-sugar coating. They're sure to be a hit with family and friends!

Oatmeal Raisin Cookies

Ingredients:

- 1 cup (2 sticks) unsalted butter, softened
- 1 1/2 cups granulated sugar
- 2 large eggs
- 2 3/4 cups all-purpose flour
- 2 teaspoons cream of tartar
- 1 teaspoon baking soda
- 1/4 teaspoon salt

For rolling:

- 1/4 cup granulated sugar
- 2 tablespoons ground cinnamon

Instructions:

1. Preheat the Oven:
    - Preheat your oven to 375°F (190°C). Line baking sheets with parchment paper or silicone baking mats.
2. Cream Butter and Sugar:
    - In a large mixing bowl, cream together the softened butter and 1 1/2 cups of granulated sugar until light and fluffy, about 2-3 minutes.
3. Add Eggs:
    - Beat in the eggs, one at a time, until well combined.
4. Combine Dry Ingredients:
    - In a separate bowl, whisk together the all-purpose flour, cream of tartar, baking soda, and salt.
5. Mix Wet and Dry Ingredients:
    - Gradually add the dry ingredients to the wet ingredients, mixing until just combined. Be careful not to overmix.
6. Prepare Rolling Mixture:
    - In a small bowl, mix together the remaining 1/4 cup of granulated sugar and ground cinnamon.
7. Form Dough Balls:
    - Roll the dough into balls, about 1 to 1 1/2 inches in diameter.

- Roll each dough ball in the cinnamon-sugar mixture until coated evenly.
8. Place on Baking Sheets:
    - Place the coated dough balls onto the prepared baking sheets, spacing them about 2 inches apart.
9. Bake the Cookies:
    - Bake in the preheated oven for 8 to 10 minutes, or until the edges are set and the tops are just beginning to crack.
    - Remove from the oven and let the cookies cool on the baking sheets for a few minutes before transferring them to wire racks to cool completely.
10. Enjoy:
    - Once cooled, serve and enjoy these delicious homemade snickerdoodle cookies!

These snickerdoodles are soft, chewy, and have a perfect balance of sweetness and spice from the cinnamon-sugar coating. They're sure to be a hit with family and friends!

Oatmeal Raisin Cookies

Here's a classic recipe for homemade oatmeal raisin cookies:

Ingredients:

- 1 cup (2 sticks) unsalted butter, softened
- 1 cup packed light brown sugar
- 1/2 cup granulated sugar
- 2 large eggs
- 1 teaspoon vanilla extract
- 1 1/2 cups all-purpose flour
- 1 teaspoon baking soda
- 1 teaspoon ground cinnamon
- 1/2 teaspoon salt
- 3 cups old-fashioned rolled oats
- 1 cup raisins

Instructions:

1. Preheat the Oven:
    - Preheat your oven to 350°F (175°C). Line baking sheets with parchment paper or silicone baking mats.
2. Cream Butter and Sugars:
    - In a large mixing bowl, cream together the softened butter, brown sugar, and granulated sugar until light and fluffy, about 2-3 minutes.
3. Add Eggs and Vanilla:
    - Beat in the eggs, one at a time, until well combined. Mix in the vanilla extract.
4. Combine Dry Ingredients:
    - In a separate bowl, whisk together the all-purpose flour, baking soda, ground cinnamon, and salt.
5. Mix Wet and Dry Ingredients:
    - Gradually add the dry ingredients to the wet ingredients, mixing until just combined.
    - Stir in the rolled oats and raisins until evenly distributed throughout the dough.
6. Form Dough Balls:

- Drop rounded tablespoons of dough onto the prepared baking sheets, spacing them about 2 inches apart.
7. Flatten Dough Balls (optional):
    - If desired, gently flatten each dough ball with the back of a spoon or the palm of your hand to create a slightly flattened cookie shape.
8. Bake the Cookies:
    - Bake in the preheated oven for 10 to 12 minutes, or until the edges are golden brown and the centers are set.
9. Cool and Serve:
    - Remove from the oven and let the cookies cool on the baking sheets for a few minutes before transferring them to wire racks to cool completely.
10. Enjoy:
    - Once cooled, serve and enjoy these delicious homemade oatmeal raisin cookies with a glass of milk or your favorite hot beverage!

These oatmeal raisin cookies are soft, chewy, and full of comforting flavors. They're perfect for enjoying as a snack or dessert any time of day!

Apple Crisp

Ingredients:

For the apple filling:

- 6 cups apples, peeled, cored, and sliced (such as Granny Smith, Honeycrisp, or Fuji)
- 1/4 cup granulated sugar
- 1 tablespoon all-purpose flour
- 1 teaspoon ground cinnamon
- 1/4 teaspoon ground nutmeg
- 1 tablespoon lemon juice
- Zest of 1 lemon

For the crisp topping:

- 1 cup old-fashioned rolled oats
- 1/2 cup all-purpose flour
- 1/2 cup packed brown sugar
- 1/2 teaspoon ground cinnamon
- 1/4 teaspoon salt
- 1/2 cup (1 stick) unsalted butter, cold and cut into small pieces

Instructions:

1. Preheat the Oven:
    - Preheat your oven to 375°F (190°C). Grease a 9x13-inch baking dish or a similar-sized baking dish.
2. Prepare the Apple Filling:
    - In a large mixing bowl, combine the sliced apples, granulated sugar, all-purpose flour, ground cinnamon, ground nutmeg, lemon juice, and lemon zest. Toss until the apples are evenly coated.
3. Transfer to Baking Dish:
    - Pour the apple mixture into the prepared baking dish, spreading it out evenly.
4. Make the Crisp Topping:
    - In a separate mixing bowl, combine the rolled oats, all-purpose flour, brown sugar, ground cinnamon, and salt.

- Cut in the cold butter pieces using a pastry cutter or fork until the mixture resembles coarse crumbs.
5. Add Topping to the Apple Mixture:
    - Sprinkle the crisp topping evenly over the apple mixture in the baking dish, covering it completely.
6. Bake the Apple Crisp:
    - Bake in the preheated oven for 40 to 45 minutes, or until the topping is golden brown and the apples are tender and bubbling.
7. Cool and Serve:
    - Remove the apple crisp from the oven and let it cool for a few minutes before serving.
    - Serve warm, topped with a scoop of vanilla ice cream or a dollop of whipped cream, if desired.
8. Enjoy:
    - Once cooled slightly, serve and enjoy this delicious homemade apple crisp, perfect for autumn gatherings or any time you're craving a comforting dessert!

This apple crisp is full of warm, cozy flavors and has a delightful crunchy topping that pairs perfectly with the tender, cinnamon-spiced apples.

Chocolate Brownies

Ingredients:

- 1 cup (2 sticks) unsalted butter, softened
- 1 cup packed light brown sugar
- 1/2 cup granulated sugar
- 2 large eggs
- 1 teaspoon vanilla extract
- 1 1/2 cups all-purpose flour
- 1 teaspoon baking soda
- 1 teaspoon ground cinnamon
- 1/2 teaspoon salt
- 3 cups old-fashioned rolled oats
- 1 cup raisins

Instructions:

1. Preheat the Oven:
    - Preheat your oven to 350°F (175°C). Line baking sheets with parchment paper or silicone baking mats.
2. Cream Butter and Sugars:
    - In a large mixing bowl, cream together the softened butter, brown sugar, and granulated sugar until light and fluffy, about 2-3 minutes.
3. Add Eggs and Vanilla:
    - Beat in the eggs, one at a time, until well combined. Mix in the vanilla extract.
4. Combine Dry Ingredients:
    - In a separate bowl, whisk together the all-purpose flour, baking soda, ground cinnamon, and salt.
5. Mix Wet and Dry Ingredients:
    - Gradually add the dry ingredients to the wet ingredients, mixing until just combined.
    - Stir in the rolled oats and raisins until evenly distributed throughout the dough.
6. Form Dough Balls:
    - Drop rounded tablespoons of dough onto the prepared baking sheets, spacing them about 2 inches apart.
7. Flatten Dough Balls (optional):
    - If desired, gently flatten each dough ball with the back of a spoon or the palm of your hand to create a slightly flattened cookie shape.
8. Bake the Cookies:
    - Bake in the preheated oven for 10 to 12 minutes, or until the edges are golden brown and the centers are set.
9. Cool and Serve:

- Remove from the oven and let the cookies cool on the baking sheets for a few minutes before transferring them to wire racks to cool completely.

10. Enjoy:
    - Once cooled, serve and enjoy these delicious homemade oatmeal raisin cookies with a glass of milk or your favorite hot beverage!

These oatmeal raisin cookies are soft, chewy, and full of comforting flavors. They're perfect for enjoying as a snack or dessert any time of day!

Apple Crisp

Here's a comforting recipe for apple crisp, a delightful dessert perfect for cool evenings:

Ingredients:

For the apple filling:

- 6 cups apples, peeled, cored, and sliced (such as Granny Smith, Honeycrisp, or Fuji)
- 1/4 cup granulated sugar
- 1 tablespoon all-purpose flour
- 1 teaspoon ground cinnamon
- 1/4 teaspoon ground nutmeg
- 1 tablespoon lemon juice
- Zest of 1 lemon

For the crisp topping:

- 1 cup old-fashioned rolled oats
- 1/2 cup all-purpose flour
- 1/2 cup packed brown sugar
- 1/2 teaspoon ground cinnamon
- 1/4 teaspoon salt
- 1/2 cup (1 stick) unsalted butter, cold and cut into small pieces

Instructions:

1. Preheat the Oven:
    - Preheat your oven to 375°F (190°C). Grease a 9x13-inch baking dish or a similar-sized baking dish.
2. Prepare the Apple Filling:
    - In a large mixing bowl, combine the sliced apples, granulated sugar, all-purpose flour, ground cinnamon, ground nutmeg, lemon juice, and lemon zest. Toss until the apples are evenly coated.
3. Transfer to Baking Dish:
    - Pour the apple mixture into the prepared baking dish, spreading it out evenly.
4. Make the Crisp Topping:
    - In a separate mixing bowl, combine the rolled oats, all-purpose flour, brown sugar, ground cinnamon, and salt.
    - Cut in the cold butter pieces using a pastry cutter or fork until the mixture resembles coarse crumbs.
5. Add Topping to the Apple Mixture:

- Sprinkle the crisp topping evenly over the apple mixture in the baking dish, covering it completely.
6. Bake the Apple Crisp:
    - Bake in the preheated oven for 40 to 45 minutes, or until the topping is golden brown and the apples are tender and bubbling.
7. Cool and Serve:
    - Remove the apple crisp from the oven and let it cool for a few minutes before serving.
    - Serve warm, topped with a scoop of vanilla ice cream or a dollop of whipped cream, if desired.
8. Enjoy:
    - Once cooled slightly, serve and enjoy this delicious homemade apple crisp, perfect for autumn gatherings or any time you're craving a comforting dessert!

This apple crisp is full of warm, cozy flavors and has a delightful crunchy topping that pairs perfectly with the tender, cinnamon-spiced apples.

Chocolate Brownies

Here's a classic recipe for homemade chocolate brownies:

Ingredients:

- 1 cup (2 sticks) unsalted butter
- 2 cups granulated sugar
- 4 large eggs
- 1 teaspoon vanilla extract
- 1 cup all-purpose flour
- 3/4 cup unsweetened cocoa powder
- 1/2 teaspoon salt
- 1/2 teaspoon baking powder

Optional Add-Ins:

- 1 cup chopped nuts (such as walnuts or pecans)
- 1 cup chocolate chips

Instructions:

1. Preheat the Oven:
    - Preheat your oven to 350°F (175°C). Grease a 9x13-inch baking pan or line it with parchment paper.
2. Melt the Butter:
    - In a saucepan or in the microwave, melt the butter until completely melted. Allow it to cool slightly.
3. Mix Wet Ingredients:
    - In a large mixing bowl, combine the melted butter and granulated sugar. Stir until well combined.
    - Add the eggs one at a time, mixing well after each addition.
    - Stir in the vanilla extract until smooth.
4. Add Dry Ingredients:
    - In a separate bowl, sift together the all-purpose flour, cocoa powder, salt, and baking powder.
    - Gradually add the dry ingredients to the wet ingredients, mixing until just combined. Be careful not to overmix.
5. Add Optional Add-Ins (if desired):
    - If using nuts or chocolate chips, gently fold them into the brownie batter until evenly distributed.
6. Pour into Baking Pan:

- Pour the brownie batter into the prepared baking pan, spreading it out evenly with a spatula.
7. Bake the Brownies:
    - Bake in the preheated oven for 25 to 30 minutes, or until a toothpick inserted into the center comes out with a few moist crumbs attached.
8. Cool and Serve:
    - Remove the brownies from the oven and let them cool completely in the pan on a wire rack.
    - Once cooled, cut into squares and serve.
9. Enjoy:
    - Serve and enjoy these delicious homemade chocolate brownies as a decadent dessert or snack!

These chocolate brownies are rich, fudgy, and full of chocolate flavor. They're perfect for satisfying any chocolate craving and are sure to be a hit with family and friends!

Pumpkin Bread

Ingredients:

- 1 3/4 cups all-purpose flour
- 1 teaspoon baking soda
- 1/2 teaspoon baking powder
- 1 teaspoon ground cinnamon
- 1/2 teaspoon ground nutmeg
- 1/2 teaspoon ground cloves
- 1/2 teaspoon salt
- 1/2 cup unsalted butter, melted
- 1 cup granulated sugar
- 1/2 cup packed light brown sugar
- 2 large eggs
- 1 (15-ounce) can pumpkin puree (about 1 3/4 cups)
- 1 teaspoon vanilla extract

Optional add-ins:

- 1/2 cup chopped nuts (such as walnuts or pecans)
- 1/2 cup chocolate chips

Instructions:

1. Preheat the Oven:
    - Preheat your oven to 350°F (175°C). Grease a 9x5-inch loaf pan or line it with parchment paper.
2. Prepare Dry Ingredients:
    - In a medium bowl, whisk together the all-purpose flour, baking soda, baking powder, ground cinnamon, ground nutmeg, ground cloves, and salt. Set aside.
3. Mix Wet Ingredients:
    - In a large mixing bowl, whisk together the melted butter, granulated sugar, and light brown sugar until well combined.
    - Add the eggs, one at a time, beating well after each addition.
    - Stir in the pumpkin puree and vanilla extract until smooth.
4. Combine Wet and Dry Ingredients:

- Gradually add the dry ingredients to the wet ingredients, stirring until just combined. Be careful not to overmix.
- If using, gently fold in the chopped nuts or chocolate chips until evenly distributed.
5. Bake the Bread:
    - Pour the batter into the prepared loaf pan, spreading it out evenly.
    - Bake in the preheated oven for 60 to 70 minutes, or until a toothpick inserted into the center comes out clean.
    - If the top of the bread starts to brown too quickly, you can tent it with aluminum foil halfway through baking.
6. Cool and Serve:
    - Remove the pumpkin bread from the oven and let it cool in the pan on a wire rack for about 10 minutes.
    - Once cooled slightly, remove the bread from the pan and let it cool completely on the wire rack before slicing and serving.
7. Enjoy:
    - Serve and enjoy slices of this delicious homemade pumpkin bread with a cup of coffee or tea, or as a snack any time of day!

This pumpkin bread is moist, flavorful, and perfect for enjoying during the autumn months. It's great for breakfast, dessert, or anytime you're craving a tasty treat!

Lemon Meringue Pie

Ingredients:

For the crust:

- 1 1/4 cups all-purpose flour
- 1/2 teaspoon salt
- 1/2 cup (1 stick) unsalted butter, cold and cut into small pieces
- 4-6 tablespoons ice water

For the lemon filling:

- 1 cup granulated sugar
- 1/4 cup cornstarch
- 1/4 teaspoon salt
- 1 1/2 cups water
- 4 large egg yolks, lightly beaten
- 1 tablespoon lemon zest
- 1/2 cup fresh lemon juice
- 2 tablespoons unsalted butter

For the meringue:

- 4 large egg whites, at room temperature
- 1/4 teaspoon cream of tartar
- 1/2 cup granulated sugar

Instructions:

1. Prepare the Crust:
    - In a large mixing bowl, whisk together the flour and salt.
    - Add the cold butter pieces to the flour mixture. Use a pastry cutter or your fingers to work the butter into the flour until the mixture resembles coarse crumbs.

- Gradually add the ice water, 1 tablespoon at a time, mixing gently with a fork until the dough comes together and forms a ball. Be careful not to overwork the dough.
- Flatten the dough into a disk, wrap it in plastic wrap, and refrigerate for at least 1 hour.

2. Preheat the Oven:
    - Preheat your oven to 375°F (190°C). Roll out the chilled dough on a lightly floured surface into a circle large enough to line a 9-inch pie dish. Carefully transfer the dough to the pie dish, gently pressing it into the bottom and up the sides. Trim any excess dough hanging over the edges. Crimp the edges as desired.
3. Blind Bake the Crust:
    - Line the chilled pie crust with parchment paper or aluminum foil and fill it with pie weights or dried beans.
    - Bake in the preheated oven for 15 minutes. Remove the parchment paper and weights, and continue baking for another 10-15 minutes, or until the crust is golden brown. Let it cool completely.
4. Prepare the Lemon Filling:
    - In a medium saucepan, whisk together the granulated sugar, cornstarch, and salt.
    - Gradually whisk in the water until smooth. Cook over medium heat, stirring constantly, until the mixture thickens and comes to a boil.
    - Boil for 1 minute, then remove from heat.
    - Gradually whisk about 1 cup of the hot sugar mixture into the beaten egg yolks to temper them.
    - Pour the tempered egg yolk mixture back into the saucepan with the remaining hot sugar mixture, whisking constantly.
    - Cook over medium heat, stirring constantly, for another 2 minutes.
    - Remove from heat and stir in the lemon zest, lemon juice, and unsalted butter until well combined.
5. Assemble the Pie:
    - Pour the lemon filling into the cooled pie crust, spreading it out evenly.
6. Prepare the Meringue:
    - In a clean mixing bowl, beat the egg whites and cream of tartar on medium speed until soft peaks form.
    - Gradually add the granulated sugar, a spoonful at a time, while continuing to beat on high speed until stiff peaks form and the sugar is dissolved.
7. Top with Meringue:

- Spread the meringue over the hot lemon filling, making sure to spread it all the way to the edges of the crust to seal it in.
8. Bake the Pie:
    - Bake in the preheated oven for 10-12 minutes, or until the meringue is golden brown.
9. Cool and Serve:
    - Remove the pie from the oven and let it cool completely on a wire rack before slicing and serving.

Enjoy the tangy lemon filling, fluffy meringue topping, and buttery crust of this delicious homemade lemon meringue pie!

Peanut Butter Brownies

Ingredients:

For the brownie layer:

- 1/2 cup (1 stick) unsalted butter
- 1 cup granulated sugar
- 2 large eggs
- 1 teaspoon vanilla extract
- 1/3 cup unsweetened cocoa powder
- 1/2 cup all-purpose flour
- 1/4 teaspoon salt
- 1/4 teaspoon baking powder

For the peanut butter layer:

- 1/2 cup creamy peanut butter
- 1/4 cup (1/2 stick) unsalted butter, melted
- 1/2 cup powdered sugar
- 1 teaspoon vanilla extract

Instructions:

1. Preheat the Oven:
    - Preheat your oven to 350°F (175°C). Grease or line an 8x8-inch baking pan with parchment paper.
2. Make the Brownie Layer:
    - In a saucepan or microwave-safe bowl, melt the butter. Remove from heat and stir in the granulated sugar until well combined.
    - Stir in the eggs, one at a time, followed by the vanilla extract.
    - In a separate bowl, sift together the cocoa powder, flour, salt, and baking powder.
    - Gradually add the dry ingredients to the wet ingredients, mixing until just combined. Be careful not to overmix.
    - Spread the brownie batter evenly into the prepared baking pan.
3. Make the Peanut Butter Layer:
    - In a mixing bowl, combine the creamy peanut butter, melted butter, powdered sugar, and vanilla extract. Mix until smooth and creamy.

        - Drop spoonfuls of the peanut butter mixture over the brownie batter in the pan.
    4. Swirl the Layers:
        - Use a knife or spatula to gently swirl the peanut butter mixture into the brownie batter, creating a marbled effect.
    5. Bake the Brownies:
        - Bake in the preheated oven for 25 to 30 minutes, or until the edges are set and a toothpick inserted into the center comes out with a few moist crumbs attached.
    6. Cool and Serve:
        - Remove the brownies from the oven and let them cool completely in the pan on a wire rack.
        - Once cooled, slice into squares and serve.

These peanut butter brownies are rich, fudgy, and full of delicious peanut butter flavor. They're perfect for satisfying your sweet cravings and are sure to be a hit with peanut butter lovers!

Coffee Cake

Ingredients:

For the cake:

- 2 cups all-purpose flour
- 1 cup granulated sugar
- 1/2 cup unsalted butter, softened
- 2 large eggs
- 1 cup sour cream
- 1 teaspoon vanilla extract
- 1 teaspoon baking powder
- 1/2 teaspoon baking soda
- 1/4 teaspoon salt

For the streusel topping:

- 1/2 cup all-purpose flour
- 1/2 cup packed light brown sugar
- 1 teaspoon ground cinnamon
- 1/4 cup unsalted butter, melted

For the glaze (optional):

- 1/2 cup powdered sugar
- 1-2 tablespoons milk or water
- 1/2 teaspoon vanilla extract

Instructions:

1. Preheat the Oven:
    - Preheat your oven to 350°F (175°C). Grease or line a 9x9-inch baking pan.
2. Make the Streusel Topping:
    - In a small mixing bowl, combine the flour, brown sugar, and cinnamon for the streusel topping.
    - Pour in the melted butter and mix until crumbly. Set aside.
3. Prepare the Cake Batter:
    - In a large mixing bowl, cream together the softened butter and granulated sugar until light and fluffy.

- Add the eggs, one at a time, beating well after each addition.
- Stir in the sour cream and vanilla extract until well combined.
4. Combine Dry Ingredients:
    - In a separate bowl, sift together the flour, baking powder, baking soda, and salt.
5. Mix Wet and Dry Ingredients:
    - Gradually add the dry ingredients to the wet ingredients, mixing until just combined. Be careful not to overmix.
6. Assemble the Cake:
    - Spread half of the cake batter into the prepared baking pan, smoothing it out evenly.
    - Sprinkle half of the streusel topping over the cake batter layer.
    - Repeat with the remaining cake batter and streusel topping, creating another layer.
7. Bake the Cake:
    - Bake in the preheated oven for 35 to 40 minutes, or until a toothpick inserted into the center comes out clean.
8. Make the Glaze (optional):
    - In a small bowl, whisk together the powdered sugar, milk or water, and vanilla extract until smooth. Adjust the consistency by adding more milk or water if needed.
9. Glaze the Cake:
    - Once the cake is done baking and has cooled slightly, drizzle the glaze over the top.
10. Serve and Enjoy:
    - Slice and serve the coffee cake warm or at room temperature.
    - Enjoy this delicious homemade coffee cake with a cup of coffee or tea for a delightful treat any time of day!

This coffee cake is moist, tender, and bursting with cinnamon flavor from the streusel topping. It's perfect for breakfast, brunch, or as a sweet snack!

Chocolate Cake

Ingredients:

For the cake:

- 1 and 3/4 cups all-purpose flour
- 3/4 cup unsweetened cocoa powder
- 2 cups granulated sugar
- 1 and 1/2 teaspoons baking powder
- 1 and 1/2 teaspoons baking soda
- 1 teaspoon salt
- 2 large eggs, at room temperature
- 1 cup whole milk
- 1/2 cup vegetable oil
- 2 teaspoons vanilla extract
- 1 cup boiling water

For the chocolate frosting:

- 1 cup unsalted butter, softened
- 3 and 1/2 cups powdered sugar
- 1/2 cup unsweetened cocoa powder
- 1/2 teaspoon salt
- 2 teaspoons vanilla extract
- 1/4 cup whole milk or heavy cream, as needed

Instructions:

1. Preheat the Oven:
    - Preheat your oven to 350°F (175°C). Grease and flour two 9-inch round cake pans.
2. Prepare the Cake Batter:
    - In a large mixing bowl, sift together the flour, cocoa powder, granulated sugar, baking powder, baking soda, and salt.
    - Add the eggs, milk, vegetable oil, and vanilla extract to the dry ingredients. Beat on medium speed until well combined.

- Reduce the speed to low and carefully mix in the boiling water until the batter is smooth. The batter will be thin.

3. **Bake the Cake:**
   - Divide the batter evenly between the prepared cake pans.
   - Bake in the preheated oven for 30 to 35 minutes, or until a toothpick inserted into the center of the cakes comes out clean.
   - Remove the cakes from the oven and let them cool in the pans for 10 minutes before transferring them to wire racks to cool completely.

4. **Make the Chocolate Frosting:**
   - In a large mixing bowl, beat the softened butter until creamy.
   - Gradually add the powdered sugar, cocoa powder, and salt, beating until well combined and smooth.
   - Beat in the vanilla extract.
   - Add the milk or heavy cream, 1 tablespoon at a time, until the frosting reaches your desired consistency.

5. **Assemble the Cake:**
   - Once the cakes are completely cool, place one layer on a serving plate or cake stand.
   - Spread a layer of frosting over the top of the first cake layer.
   - Place the second cake layer on top and frost the top and sides of the cake with the remaining frosting.

6. **Decorate (optional):**
   - Decorate the cake with chocolate shavings, sprinkles, or any other decorations of your choice.

7. **Serve and Enjoy:**
   - Slice and serve the chocolate cake at room temperature.
   - Enjoy this delicious homemade chocolate cake as a decadent dessert for any occasion!

This chocolate cake is rich, moist, and full of deep chocolate flavor. It's sure to be a hit with chocolate lovers of all ages!

Cranberry Orange Scones

Ingredients:

- 2 cups all-purpose flour
- 1/3 cup granulated sugar
- 1 tablespoon baking powder
- 1/2 teaspoon salt
- 1/2 cup (1 stick) unsalted butter, cold and cut into small pieces
- 1/2 cup dried cranberries
- Zest of 1 orange
- 1/2 cup heavy cream, plus more for brushing
- 1 large egg
- 1 teaspoon vanilla extract

For the glaze:

- 1 cup powdered sugar
- 2-3 tablespoons freshly squeezed orange juice
- Zest of 1 orange (optional)

Instructions:

1. Preheat the Oven:
    - Preheat your oven to 400°F (200°C). Line a baking sheet with parchment paper or a silicone baking mat.
2. Prepare the Dough:
    - In a large mixing bowl, whisk together the all-purpose flour, granulated sugar, baking powder, and salt.
    - Add the cold butter pieces to the flour mixture. Use a pastry cutter or your fingers to work the butter into the flour until the mixture resembles coarse crumbs.
    - Stir in the dried cranberries and orange zest until evenly distributed.
3. Mix the Wet Ingredients:
    - In a separate bowl, whisk together the heavy cream, egg, and vanilla extract until well combined.
4. Combine Wet and Dry Ingredients:

- Gradually add the wet ingredients to the dry ingredients, mixing until just combined. Be careful not to overmix.
5. Shape the Scones:
    - Turn the dough out onto a lightly floured surface and gently knead it a few times until it comes together.
    - Pat the dough into a circle about 1-inch thick.
    - Use a sharp knife or a bench scraper to cut the circle into 8 wedges.
6. Bake the Scones:
    - Transfer the scones to the prepared baking sheet, spacing them a few inches apart.
    - Lightly brush the tops of the scones with additional heavy cream.
    - Bake in the preheated oven for 15 to 18 minutes, or until the scones are golden brown and cooked through.
7. Make the Glaze:
    - In a small bowl, whisk together the powdered sugar and freshly squeezed orange juice until smooth. Add more juice if needed to reach your desired consistency.
    - Optionally, stir in some orange zest for extra flavor.
8. Glaze the Scones:
    - Once the scones are cool, drizzle the glaze over the tops.
9. Serve and Enjoy:
    - Serve the cranberry orange scones with a hot cup of tea or coffee for a delightful breakfast or afternoon treat!

These cranberry orange scones are tender, flaky, and bursting with citrus and berry flavors. They're perfect for enjoying fresh out of the oven or even as a make-ahead breakfast option!

Pineapple Upside-Down Cake

Ingredients:

For the topping:

- 1/2 cup unsalted butter
- 1 cup packed light brown sugar
- 1 can (20 ounces) pineapple slices in juice, drained
- Maraschino cherries, drained (optional)

For the cake batter:

- 1 and 1/2 cups all-purpose flour
- 1 and 1/2 teaspoons baking powder
- 1/4 teaspoon salt
- 1/2 cup unsalted butter, softened
- 1 cup granulated sugar
- 2 large eggs
- 1 teaspoon vanilla extract
- 1/2 cup pineapple juice (reserved from the canned pineapple)
- 1/4 cup milk

Instructions:

1. Preheat the Oven:
    - Preheat your oven to 350°F (175°C). Grease a 9-inch round cake pan.
2. Prepare the Topping:
    - In a small saucepan, melt the butter over medium heat.
    - Stir in the brown sugar until dissolved and the mixture is smooth.
    - Pour the mixture into the prepared cake pan and spread it out evenly.
    - Arrange the pineapple slices on top of the brown sugar mixture. You can place a cherry in the center of each pineapple slice if desired.
3. Prepare the Cake Batter:
    - In a medium bowl, whisk together the flour, baking powder, and salt.
    - In a separate large mixing bowl, cream together the softened butter and granulated sugar until light and fluffy.

- Beat in the eggs, one at a time, until well combined.
- Stir in the vanilla extract.
- Gradually add the dry ingredients to the creamed mixture, alternating with the pineapple juice and milk. Begin and end with the dry ingredients, mixing until just combined.

4. Assemble and Bake the Cake:
   - Pour the cake batter over the pineapple slices in the cake pan, spreading it out evenly.
5. Bake the Cake:
   - Bake in the preheated oven for 40 to 45 minutes, or until a toothpick inserted into the center of the cake comes out clean.
6. Cool and Invert the Cake:
   - Remove the cake from the oven and let it cool in the pan for 5 minutes.
   - Carefully invert the cake onto a serving plate while it's still warm. Leave the pan on top of the cake for a few minutes to allow the brown sugar topping to drizzle over the cake.
7. Serve and Enjoy:
   - Slice and serve the pineapple upside-down cake warm or at room temperature.
   - Enjoy this classic dessert with a dollop of whipped cream or a scoop of vanilla ice cream, if desired!

This pineapple upside-down cake is moist, flavorful, and beautifully caramelized on top, making it a perfect dessert for any occasion.

Biscuits and Gravy

Ingredients:

For the biscuits:

- 2 cups all-purpose flour
- 1 tablespoon baking powder
- 1 teaspoon granulated sugar
- 1/2 teaspoon salt
- 1/2 cup (1 stick) unsalted butter, cold and cut into small pieces
- 3/4 cup buttermilk, cold

For the sausage gravy:

- 1 pound ground breakfast sausage (mild or hot, depending on preference)
- 1/4 cup all-purpose flour
- 3 cups whole milk
- Salt and pepper, to taste

Instructions:

1. Make the Biscuits:
    - Preheat your oven to 425°F (220°C). Line a baking sheet with parchment paper.
    - In a large mixing bowl, whisk together the flour, baking powder, sugar, and salt.
    - Add the cold, cubed butter to the flour mixture. Use a pastry cutter or your fingers to work the butter into the flour until the mixture resembles coarse crumbs.
    - Gradually pour in the cold buttermilk, stirring until the dough just comes together. Be careful not to overmix.
    - Turn the dough out onto a lightly floured surface. Pat it into a rectangle about 1/2-inch thick.
    - Use a biscuit cutter or a drinking glass to cut out biscuits. Place them on the prepared baking sheet, spacing them about 2 inches apart.

- Gather any scraps of dough, pat them together, and cut out additional biscuits until all the dough is used.
- Bake the biscuits in the preheated oven for 12 to 15 minutes, or until golden brown on top.

2. Prepare the Sausage Gravy:
    - While the biscuits are baking, cook the ground breakfast sausage in a large skillet over medium heat. Break up the sausage with a spatula as it cooks, until it is browned and cooked through.
    - Sprinkle the cooked sausage with flour and stir until the flour is absorbed and the mixture is evenly coated.
    - Gradually pour in the milk, stirring constantly, until the gravy thickens and comes to a simmer.
    - Reduce the heat to low and simmer the gravy for a few minutes, stirring occasionally, until it reaches your desired consistency.
    - Season the gravy with salt and pepper to taste.

3. Serve:
    - Split the warm biscuits in half and place them on serving plates.
    - Ladle the hot sausage gravy over the biscuits.
    - Serve immediately and enjoy this comforting and hearty breakfast dish!

This biscuits and gravy recipe is a classic comfort food that's perfect for a weekend brunch or a satisfying breakfast any day of the week.

Strawberry Rhubarb Pie

Ingredients:

For the pie crust:

- 2 1/2 cups all-purpose flour
- 1 tablespoon granulated sugar
- 1 teaspoon salt
- 1 cup (2 sticks) unsalted butter, cold and cut into small cubes
- 6-8 tablespoons ice water

For the filling:

- 3 cups sliced rhubarb (about 1/2-inch pieces)
- 3 cups sliced strawberries
- 1 cup granulated sugar
- 1/4 cup cornstarch
- 1 tablespoon lemon juice
- 1 teaspoon vanilla extract
- 1/4 teaspoon ground cinnamon (optional)
- 1 egg, beaten (for egg wash)
- 1 tablespoon granulated sugar (for sprinkling)

Instructions:

1. Prepare the Pie Crust:
   - In a large mixing bowl, whisk together the flour, sugar, and salt.
   - Add the cold, cubed butter to the flour mixture. Use a pastry cutter or your fingers to work the butter into the flour until the mixture resembles coarse crumbs.
   - Gradually add the ice water, 1 tablespoon at a time, mixing gently with a fork until the dough comes together and forms a ball. Be careful not to overwork the dough.
   - Divide the dough in half, shape each half into a disk, wrap them in plastic wrap, and refrigerate for at least 30 minutes.
2. Preheat the Oven:

- Preheat your oven to 400°F (200°C). Place a baking sheet in the oven to preheat as well.
3. Prepare the Filling:
    - In a large mixing bowl, combine the sliced rhubarb, sliced strawberries, granulated sugar, cornstarch, lemon juice, vanilla extract, and ground cinnamon (if using). Toss until the fruit is evenly coated.
4. Roll out the Pie Crust:
    - On a lightly floured surface, roll out one disk of the chilled pie dough into a circle about 12 inches in diameter. Carefully transfer it to a 9-inch pie dish, gently pressing it into the bottom and up the sides.
5. Fill the Pie:
    - Pour the strawberry rhubarb filling into the prepared pie crust, spreading it out evenly.
6. Top with Second Crust:
    - Roll out the second disk of chilled pie dough into a circle about 12 inches in diameter. You can either place the dough over the filling as a full top crust, or use a lattice or other decorative design.
7. Crimp the Edges:
    - Trim any excess dough hanging over the edges of the pie dish. Fold the edges of the bottom crust over the top crust, and crimp them together using your fingers or a fork to create a decorative edge.
8. Brush with Egg Wash:
    - Brush the top crust with the beaten egg, and sprinkle it with granulated sugar for a golden, crispy finish.
9. Bake the Pie:
    - Place the pie on the preheated baking sheet in the oven.
    - Bake for 20 minutes at 400°F (200°C), then reduce the oven temperature to 350°F (175°C) and continue baking for an additional 40 to 50 minutes, or until the crust is golden brown and the filling is bubbling.
10. Cool and Serve:
    - Remove the pie from the oven and let it cool on a wire rack for at least 2 hours before slicing and serving.
    - Serve slices of this delicious homemade strawberry rhubarb pie with a scoop of vanilla ice cream or a dollop of whipped cream, if desired!

Enjoy the sweet-tart flavor combination of strawberries and rhubarb in this classic pie, with a flaky, buttery crust that's sure to impress!

Almond Biscotti

Ingredients:

- 2 cups all-purpose flour
- 1 cup granulated sugar
- 1 teaspoon baking powder
- 1/4 teaspoon salt
- 3 large eggs
- 1 teaspoon vanilla extract
- 1 teaspoon almond extract
- 1 cup whole almonds, toasted and coarsely chopped

Optional glaze:

- 1 cup powdered sugar
- 2-3 tablespoons milk or water
- 1/2 teaspoon almond extract

Instructions:

1. Preheat the Oven:
    - Preheat your oven to 350°F (175°C). Line a baking sheet with parchment paper or a silicone baking mat.
2. Toast the Almonds:
    - Spread the almonds on a baking sheet and toast them in the preheated oven for 8 to 10 minutes, or until fragrant and lightly golden. Let them cool, then coarsely chop them.
3. Prepare the Dough:
    - In a large mixing bowl, whisk together the flour, sugar, baking powder, and salt.
    - In a separate bowl, beat the eggs, vanilla extract, and almond extract together until well combined.
    - Gradually add the egg mixture to the dry ingredients, mixing until a dough forms.
    - Fold in the toasted and chopped almonds until evenly distributed.
4. Shape the Dough:

- Divide the dough in half. On a lightly floured surface, shape each half into a log about 12 inches long and 2 inches wide. Place the logs on the prepared baking sheet, spacing them a few inches apart.

5. Bake the Biscotti:
   - Bake the logs in the preheated oven for 25 to 30 minutes, or until firm and lightly golden brown.
6. Cool and Slice:
   - Remove the baking sheet from the oven and let the biscotti logs cool for about 10 minutes. Reduce the oven temperature to 325°F (160°C).
   - Transfer the cooled logs to a cutting board and use a serrated knife to slice them diagonally into 1/2-inch thick pieces.
7. Bake Again:
   - Place the sliced biscotti cut-side down on the baking sheet. Bake for an additional 10 to 15 minutes, or until the biscotti are golden brown and crisp.
   - Remove from the oven and let them cool completely on a wire rack.
8. Optional Glaze:
   - If desired, whisk together the powdered sugar, milk or water, and almond extract until smooth. Drizzle the glaze over the cooled biscotti and let it set before serving.
9. Serve and Enjoy:
   - Serve these delicious homemade almond biscotti with a cup of coffee or tea for a delightful treat any time of day!

These almond biscotti are crunchy, full of almond flavor, and perfect for dipping into your favorite hot beverage. Enjoy them as a sweet snack or give them as gifts to friends and family!

Eclairs

Ingredients:

For the choux pastry:

- 1/2 cup water
- 1/2 cup whole milk
- 1/2 cup (1 stick) unsalted butter, cut into cubes
- 1 tablespoon granulated sugar
- 1/4 teaspoon salt
- 1 cup all-purpose flour
- 4 large eggs

For the filling:

- 1 1/2 cups whole milk
- 1/2 cup granulated sugar
- 4 large egg yolks
- 1/4 cup cornstarch
- 1 teaspoon vanilla extract
- 1 cup heavy cream, chilled

For the chocolate glaze:

- 1/2 cup semisweet chocolate chips
- 1/4 cup heavy cream

Instructions:

1. Make the Choux Pastry:
    - Preheat your oven to 400°F (200°C). Line a baking sheet with parchment paper.
    - In a saucepan, combine the water, milk, butter, sugar, and salt. Bring to a boil over medium heat.
    - Reduce the heat to low and add the flour all at once. Stir vigorously until the mixture forms a smooth dough and pulls away from the sides of the pan.
    - Remove from heat and let the mixture cool for a few minutes.

- Add the eggs, one at a time, beating well after each addition, until the dough is smooth and glossy.
2. Pipe the Éclairs:
    - Transfer the choux pastry dough to a piping bag fitted with a large round tip.
    - Pipe the dough into 4-inch-long strips onto the prepared baking sheet, leaving space between each éclair.
    - Use a damp finger to smooth out any peaks or bumps on the surface of the dough.
3. Bake the Éclairs:
    - Place the baking sheet in the preheated oven and immediately reduce the temperature to 375°F (190°C).
    - Bake for 25 to 30 minutes, or until the éclairs are puffed, golden brown, and crisp.
    - Remove from the oven and let them cool completely on a wire rack.
4. Make the Filling:
    - In a saucepan, heat the milk over medium heat until it just begins to simmer.
    - In a separate bowl, whisk together the sugar, egg yolks, and cornstarch until pale and thick.
    - Gradually pour the hot milk into the egg mixture, whisking constantly.
    - Return the mixture to the saucepan and cook over medium heat, stirring constantly, until thickened.
    - Remove from heat and stir in the vanilla extract. Transfer the mixture to a bowl and cover it with plastic wrap, pressing the plastic wrap directly onto the surface of the custard to prevent a skin from forming.
    - Let the custard cool to room temperature.
5. Fill the Éclairs:
    - Once the custard has cooled, whip the chilled heavy cream until stiff peaks form.
    - Gently fold the whipped cream into the custard until well combined.
    - Transfer the filling to a piping bag fitted with a small round tip.
    - Insert the tip of the piping bag into one end of each éclair and pipe the filling inside until full.
6. Make the Chocolate Glaze:
    - In a heatproof bowl, combine the chocolate chips and heavy cream.
    - Microwave in 30-second intervals, stirring between each interval, until the chocolate is melted and the mixture is smooth.
7. Glaze the Éclairs:

- Dip the top of each filled éclair into the chocolate glaze, allowing any excess to drip off.
- Place the glazed éclairs on a wire rack set over a baking sheet to set.

8. Serve and Enjoy:
    - Once the glaze has set, serve the éclairs immediately or store them in the refrigerator until ready to serve.
    - Enjoy these delicious homemade éclairs as a decadent dessert or sweet treat!

These éclairs are sure to impress with their light and airy pastry, creamy filling, and rich chocolate glaze. Enjoy making and sharing them with friends and family!

Baklava

Ingredients:

For the filling:

- 1 pound (about 4 cups) mixed nuts (such as walnuts, pistachios, and almonds), finely chopped
- 1/2 cup granulated sugar
- 1 teaspoon ground cinnamon
- 1/4 teaspoon ground cloves
- 1/4 teaspoon ground nutmeg
- 1 cup unsalted butter, melted

For the phyllo dough layers:

- 1 pound phyllo dough, thawed if frozen
- 1 cup unsalted butter, melted

For the syrup:

- 1 cup granulated sugar
- 1 cup water
- 1/2 cup honey
- 1 cinnamon stick
- 4 whole cloves
- 1 strip of lemon peel

Instructions:

1. Prepare the Filling:
    - In a mixing bowl, combine the finely chopped nuts, granulated sugar, ground cinnamon, ground cloves, and ground nutmeg. Mix well and set aside.
2. Prepare the Phyllo Dough:
    - Preheat your oven to 350°F (175°C). Grease a 9x13-inch baking dish.

- Unroll the phyllo dough and cover it with a damp towel to prevent it from drying out.
- Brush the bottom of the baking dish with melted butter.
- Place one sheet of phyllo dough in the baking dish and brush it with melted butter. Repeat this process, layering the phyllo dough and brushing each layer with melted butter, until you have used about half of the phyllo dough.

3. Add the Nut Filling:
   - Spread the nut filling evenly over the layer of phyllo dough in the baking dish.
4. Continue Layering:
   - Continue layering the remaining phyllo dough sheets on top of the nut filling, brushing each layer with melted butter.
5. Cut and Score:
   - Using a sharp knife, carefully cut the baklava into squares or diamond shapes. Be careful not to cut all the way through to the bottom of the baking dish.
6. Bake the Baklava:
   - Place the baking dish in the preheated oven and bake for 50 to 60 minutes, or until the baklava is golden brown and crisp.
7. Make the Syrup:
   - While the baklava is baking, prepare the syrup. In a saucepan, combine the granulated sugar, water, honey, cinnamon stick, whole cloves, and lemon peel.
   - Bring the mixture to a boil over medium heat, stirring occasionally. Reduce the heat to low and simmer for 10 to 15 minutes, or until the syrup has thickened slightly.
   - Remove the saucepan from heat and let the syrup cool slightly.
8. Pour the Syrup:
   - Once the baklava is done baking, remove it from the oven and immediately pour the syrup evenly over the hot baklava.
9. Cool and Serve:
   - Let the baklava cool completely in the baking dish before serving.
   - Enjoy this delicious homemade baklava as a sweet treat or dessert!

Baklava is a classic Mediterranean dessert known for its flaky layers of phyllo dough and rich nut filling, soaked in sweet syrup. This homemade version is sure to impress with its crunchy texture and aromatic flavors!

Rugelach

Here's a recipe for homemade rugelach, a delightful Jewish pastry filled with sweet fillings:

Ingredients:

For the dough:

- 1 cup unsalted butter, softened
- 8 ounces cream cheese, softened
- 1/4 cup granulated sugar
- 2 cups all-purpose flour
- 1/4 teaspoon salt

For the filling:

- 1/2 cup packed brown sugar
- 1 tablespoon ground cinnamon
- 1/2 cup finely chopped walnuts or pecans
- 1/2 cup raisins or currants
- 1/4 cup apricot preserves (or raspberry jam)

For the topping:

- 1 egg, beaten
- 2 tablespoons granulated sugar
- 1 teaspoon ground cinnamon

Instructions:

1. Prepare the Dough:
    - In a large mixing bowl, beat together the softened butter, cream cheese, and granulated sugar until smooth and creamy.
    - Gradually add the flour and salt to the butter mixture, mixing until a soft dough forms.
    - Divide the dough into 4 equal portions, shape each portion into a disk, wrap them in plastic wrap, and refrigerate for at least 1 hour or until firm.
2. Prepare the Filling:

- In a small mixing bowl, combine the brown sugar and ground cinnamon for the filling.
- Stir in the finely chopped nuts and raisins or currants until evenly distributed.
- Set aside.
3. Assemble the Rugelach:
    - Preheat your oven to 350°F (175°C). Line a baking sheet with parchment paper.
    - Take one disk of chilled dough out of the refrigerator. On a lightly floured surface, roll out the dough into a circle about 1/8 inch thick.
    - Spread a thin layer of apricot preserves or raspberry jam over the rolled-out dough, leaving a small border around the edges.
    - Sprinkle the cinnamon sugar-nut mixture evenly over the jam-covered dough.
4. Cut and Shape the Rugelach:
    - Using a sharp knife or pizza cutter, cut the dough into 8 equal wedges, like a pizza.
    - Starting from the wide end, roll up each wedge tightly to form a crescent shape.
    - Place the rolled rugelach on the prepared baking sheet, seam side down. Repeat this process with the remaining dough and filling.
5. Brush with Egg Wash:
    - In a small bowl, beat the egg. Brush the tops of the rugelach with the beaten egg.
6. Sprinkle with Cinnamon Sugar:
    - In another small bowl, mix together the granulated sugar and ground cinnamon for the topping.
    - Sprinkle the cinnamon sugar mixture evenly over the tops of the rugelach.
7. Bake the Rugelach:
    - Bake in the preheated oven for 20 to 25 minutes, or until golden brown and fragrant.
8. Cool and Serve:
    - Remove the rugelach from the oven and let them cool on the baking sheet for a few minutes before transferring them to a wire rack to cool completely.
    - Enjoy these delicious homemade rugelach as a sweet treat or dessert!

Rugelach are wonderfully flaky and buttery pastries with a deliciously sweet filling. They make a perfect addition to holiday gatherings or any occasion where you want to enjoy a delightful pastry!

Texas Sheet Cake

Ingredients:

For the cake:

- 2 cups all-purpose flour
- 2 cups granulated sugar
- 1 teaspoon baking soda
- 1/2 teaspoon salt
- 1 cup unsalted butter
- 1 cup water
- 1/4 cup unsweetened cocoa powder
- 2 large eggs
- 1/2 cup buttermilk
- 2 teaspoons vanilla extract

For the frosting:

- 1/2 cup unsalted butter
- 1/4 cup unsweetened cocoa powder
- 1/4 cup milk
- 1 teaspoon vanilla extract
- 4 cups powdered sugar
- 1 cup chopped pecans or walnuts (optional)

Instructions:

1. Preheat the Oven and Prepare the Pan:
    - Preheat your oven to 350°F (175°C). Grease and flour a 18x13-inch rimmed baking sheet.
2. Make the Cake:
    - In a large mixing bowl, whisk together the flour, sugar, baking soda, and salt.
    - In a medium saucepan, combine the butter, water, and cocoa powder. Bring to a boil over medium heat, stirring constantly.

- Pour the hot butter mixture over the dry ingredients and mix until well combined.
- In a separate bowl, whisk together the eggs, buttermilk, and vanilla extract. Add this mixture to the batter and mix until smooth.
- Pour the batter into the prepared baking sheet and spread it out evenly.

3. Bake the Cake:
    - Bake in the preheated oven for 20 to 25 minutes, or until a toothpick inserted into the center comes out clean.
4. Make the Frosting:
    - About 5 minutes before the cake is done baking, start preparing the frosting.
    - In a medium saucepan, combine the butter, cocoa powder, and milk. Bring to a boil over medium heat, stirring constantly.
    - Remove the saucepan from the heat and stir in the vanilla extract and powdered sugar until smooth.
    - Stir in the chopped nuts, if using.
5. Frost the Cake:
    - As soon as the cake comes out of the oven, pour the warm frosting over the hot cake and spread it out evenly with a spatula.
6. Cool and Serve:
    - Let the cake cool completely in the pan before slicing and serving.
    - Enjoy this classic Texas sheet cake as a delicious dessert or sweet treat!

Texas sheet cake is known for its moist texture, rich chocolate flavor, and decadent frosting. It's a crowd-pleasing dessert that's perfect for potlucks, parties, or any occasion where you want to enjoy a slice of delicious homemade cake.

Whoopie Pies

Ingredients:

For the cookies:

- 2 cups all-purpose flour
- 1/2 cup unsweetened cocoa powder
- 1 teaspoon baking powder
- 1/2 teaspoon baking soda
- 1/2 teaspoon salt
- 1/2 cup unsalted butter, softened
- 1 cup granulated sugar
- 1 large egg
- 1 teaspoon vanilla extract
- 1 cup buttermilk

For the filling:

- 1/2 cup unsalted butter, softened
- 1 cup powdered sugar
- 1 teaspoon vanilla extract
- 1 (7-ounce) jar marshmallow creme

Instructions:

1. Preheat the Oven:
   - Preheat your oven to 350°F (175°C). Line baking sheets with parchment paper.
2. Make the Cookies:
   - In a medium bowl, whisk together the flour, cocoa powder, baking powder, baking soda, and salt.
   - In a large mixing bowl, cream together the softened butter and granulated sugar until light and fluffy.
   - Add the egg and vanilla extract to the butter mixture, beating until well combined.

- Gradually add the dry ingredients to the wet ingredients, alternating with the buttermilk, mixing until just combined.
- Drop spoonfuls of batter onto the prepared baking sheets, spacing them about 2 inches apart.
- Bake in the preheated oven for 10 to 12 minutes, or until the cookies are set and slightly firm to the touch.
- Remove from the oven and let the cookies cool on the baking sheets for a few minutes before transferring them to wire racks to cool completely.

3. Make the Filling:
   - In a mixing bowl, beat the softened butter until creamy.
   - Gradually add the powdered sugar and vanilla extract, beating until smooth and well combined.
   - Add the marshmallow creme and beat until the filling is light and fluffy.
4. Assemble the Whoopie Pies:
   - Once the cookies are completely cooled, spread a generous amount of filling onto the flat side of one cookie.
   - Top with another cookie, flat side down, to create a sandwich.
   - Repeat with the remaining cookies and filling.
5. Serve and Enjoy:
   - Serve these delicious homemade whoopie pies immediately, or store them in an airtight container at room temperature for up to 3 days.

These whoopie pies are soft, cake-like cookies filled with a creamy, marshmallow-flavored filling. They're perfect for enjoying as a sweet treat or dessert, and they're sure to be a hit with friends and family!

Danish Pastries

Ingredients:

For the dough:

- 2 and 1/4 teaspoons (1 packet) active dry yeast
- 1/4 cup warm water (about 110°F or 45°C)
- 1/2 cup milk, warmed
- 1/4 cup granulated sugar
- 1/2 teaspoon salt
- 1 large egg, beaten
- 2 and 1/2 cups all-purpose flour
- 1 cup (2 sticks) unsalted butter, cold

For the filling and topping:

- Your choice of fillings such as jam, pastry cream, almond paste, or chocolate
- Sliced fruit or nuts (optional)
- Powdered sugar for dusting (optional)
- Glaze (optional)

Instructions:

1. Activate the Yeast:
    - In a small bowl, dissolve the yeast in warm water and let it sit for 5-10 minutes until frothy.
2. Prepare the Dough:
    - In a large mixing bowl, combine the warm milk, sugar, salt, and beaten egg.
    - Add the activated yeast mixture and stir until well combined.
    - Gradually add the flour, stirring until a soft dough forms.
    - Turn the dough out onto a lightly floured surface and knead it for about 5 minutes until smooth and elastic.
    - Shape the dough into a ball and place it in a lightly greased bowl. Cover with a clean kitchen towel or plastic wrap and let it rise in a warm, draft-free place for about 1 hour or until doubled in size.
3. Prepare the Butter Block:

- While the dough is rising, prepare the butter block. Place the cold butter between two sheets of parchment paper and pound it with a rolling pin to flatten and soften it into a rectangle about 1/2 inch thick. Refrigerate until firm.

4. Laminate the Dough:
    - Once the dough has doubled in size, punch it down and roll it out on a lightly floured surface into a rectangle about 1/4 inch thick.
    - Place the chilled butter block in the center of the dough rectangle and fold the dough over the butter, enclosing it completely.
    - Roll out the dough into a larger rectangle, then fold it into thirds like a letter (this is called a single turn). Wrap the dough in plastic wrap and refrigerate for 30 minutes.
    - Repeat the rolling, folding, and chilling process two more times (for a total of three turns). This creates layers in the dough, resulting in a flaky texture.

5. Shape and Fill the Danish:
    - After the final turn, roll out the dough into a large rectangle about 1/4 inch thick.
    - Cut the dough into squares or rectangles, depending on the size and shape of pastries you want to make.
    - Place a spoonful of filling in the center of each dough piece. Add sliced fruit or nuts if desired.
    - Fold the corners or sides of the dough over the filling to create a pocket or envelope shape.

6. Proof and Bake:
    - Place the shaped pastries on a parchment-lined baking sheet, leaving space between them to rise.
    - Cover the pastries loosely with plastic wrap and let them rise in a warm place for about 30-45 minutes until puffy.
    - Preheat your oven to 375°F (190°C).
    - Once the pastries have risen, bake them in the preheated oven for 15-20 minutes or until golden brown and puffed.

7. Finish and Serve:
    - Remove the pastries from the oven and let them cool on a wire rack.
    - Optionally, drizzle the pastries with glaze and dust with powdered sugar before serving.

Enjoy your homemade Danish pastries with a cup of coffee or tea for a delightful breakfast or snack!

Lemon Pound Cake

Ingredients:

For the dough:

- 2 and 1/4 teaspoons (1 packet) active dry yeast
- 1/4 cup warm water (about 110°F or 45°C)
- 1/2 cup milk, warmed
- 1/4 cup granulated sugar
- 1/2 teaspoon salt
- 1 large egg, beaten
- 2 and 1/2 cups all-purpose flour
- 1 cup (2 sticks) unsalted butter, cold

For the filling and topping:

- Your choice of fillings such as jam, pastry cream, almond paste, or chocolate
- Sliced fruit or nuts (optional)
- Powdered sugar for dusting (optional)
- Glaze (optional)

Instructions:

1. Activate the Yeast:
    - In a small bowl, dissolve the yeast in warm water and let it sit for 5-10 minutes until frothy.
2. Prepare the Dough:
    - In a large mixing bowl, combine the warm milk, sugar, salt, and beaten egg.
    - Add the activated yeast mixture and stir until well combined.
    - Gradually add the flour, stirring until a soft dough forms.
    - Turn the dough out onto a lightly floured surface and knead it for about 5 minutes until smooth and elastic.
    - Shape the dough into a ball and place it in a lightly greased bowl. Cover with a clean kitchen towel or plastic wrap and let it rise in a warm, draft-free place for about 1 hour or until doubled in size.
3. Prepare the Butter Block:
    - While the dough is rising, prepare the butter block. Place the cold butter between two sheets of parchment paper and pound it with a rolling pin to flatten and soften it into a rectangle about 1/2 inch thick. Refrigerate until firm.
4. Laminate the Dough:

- Once the dough has doubled in size, punch it down and roll it out on a lightly floured surface into a rectangle about 1/4 inch thick.
- Place the chilled butter block in the center of the dough rectangle and fold the dough over the butter, enclosing it completely.
- Roll out the dough into a larger rectangle, then fold it into thirds like a letter (this is called a single turn). Wrap the dough in plastic wrap and refrigerate for 30 minutes.
- Repeat the rolling, folding, and chilling process two more times (for a total of three turns). This creates layers in the dough, resulting in a flaky texture.

5. Shape and Fill the Danish:
    - After the final turn, roll out the dough into a large rectangle about 1/4 inch thick.
    - Cut the dough into squares or rectangles, depending on the size and shape of pastries you want to make.
    - Place a spoonful of filling in the center of each dough piece. Add sliced fruit or nuts if desired.
    - Fold the corners or sides of the dough over the filling to create a pocket or envelope shape.
6. Proof and Bake:
    - Place the shaped pastries on a parchment-lined baking sheet, leaving space between them to rise.
    - Cover the pastries loosely with plastic wrap and let them rise in a warm place for about 30-45 minutes until puffy.
    - Preheat your oven to 375°F (190°C).
    - Once the pastries have risen, bake them in the preheated oven for 15-20 minutes or until golden brown and puffed.
7. Finish and Serve:
    - Remove the pastries from the oven and let them cool on a wire rack.
    - Optionally, drizzle the pastries with glaze and dust with powdered sugar before serving.

Enjoy your homemade Danish pastries with a cup of coffee or tea for a delightful breakfast or snack!

Lemon Pound Cake

Here's a recipe for a delicious lemon pound cake:

Ingredients:

For the cake:

- 1 cup (2 sticks) unsalted butter, softened
- 2 cups granulated sugar
- 4 large eggs, room temperature
- 1/4 cup fresh lemon juice
- 2 tablespoons lemon zest (from about 2 lemons)
- 3 cups all-purpose flour
- 1/2 teaspoon baking powder
- 1/2 teaspoon baking soda
- 1/2 teaspoon salt
- 1 cup plain yogurt or sour cream
- 1 teaspoon vanilla extract

For the glaze:

- 1 cup powdered sugar
- 2-3 tablespoons fresh lemon juice
- 1 tablespoon lemon zest (optional)

Instructions:

1. Preheat the Oven:
    - Preheat your oven to 350°F (175°C). Grease and flour a 9x5-inch loaf pan.
2. Make the Cake:
    - In a large mixing bowl, cream together the softened butter and granulated sugar until light and fluffy.
    - Add the eggs one at a time, beating well after each addition.
    - Mix in the lemon juice and lemon zest until well combined.
3. Prepare the Dry Ingredients:
    - In a separate bowl, whisk together the flour, baking powder, baking soda, and salt.
4. Combine Wet and Dry Ingredients:
    - Gradually add the dry ingredients to the wet ingredients, alternating with the yogurt or sour cream, beginning and ending with the flour mixture. Mix until just combined.
    - Stir in the vanilla extract.
5. Bake the Cake:

- Pour the batter into the prepared loaf pan and smooth the top with a spatula.
- Bake in the preheated oven for 50 to 60 minutes, or until a toothpick inserted into the center comes out clean.
- If the top of the cake starts to brown too quickly, you can tent it with aluminum foil halfway through baking to prevent over-browning.

6. Cool the Cake:
    - Remove the cake from the oven and let it cool in the pan for about 10 minutes.
    - Carefully remove the cake from the pan and transfer it to a wire rack to cool completely.
7. Make the Glaze:
    - In a small bowl, whisk together the powdered sugar and fresh lemon juice until smooth. Add more lemon juice if needed to reach your desired consistency.
    - Stir in the lemon zest, if using.
8. Glaze the Cake:
    - Once the cake has cooled, drizzle the glaze over the top of the cake.
    - Allow the glaze to set for a few minutes before slicing and serving.

Enjoy slices of this delicious homemade lemon pound cake with a cup of tea or coffee for a delightful treat any time of day!

Fig Newtons

Ingredients:

For the dough:

- 1 cup (2 sticks) unsalted butter, softened
- 1 cup granulated sugar
- 2 large eggs
- 1 teaspoon vanilla extract
- 2 and 1/2 cups all-purpose flour
- 1/2 teaspoon baking powder
- 1/2 teaspoon salt

For the fig filling:

- 2 cups dried figs, stems removed and chopped
- 1/2 cup water
- 1/4 cup granulated sugar
- Zest and juice of 1 lemon
- 1/2 teaspoon ground cinnamon
- Pinch of salt

Instructions:

1. Make the Fig Filling:
    - In a saucepan, combine the chopped dried figs, water, granulated sugar, lemon zest, lemon juice, ground cinnamon, and a pinch of salt.
    - Bring the mixture to a simmer over medium heat, then reduce the heat to low and cook for about 10 minutes, stirring occasionally, until the figs are soft and the mixture has thickened.
    - Remove from heat and let the fig filling cool slightly. Transfer it to a food processor or blender and pulse until smooth. Set aside to cool completely.
2. Prepare the Dough:
    - In a large mixing bowl, cream together the softened butter and granulated sugar until light and fluffy.

- Add the eggs, one at a time, beating well after each addition. Stir in the vanilla extract.
- In a separate bowl, whisk together the all-purpose flour, baking powder, and salt.
- Gradually add the dry ingredients to the butter mixture, mixing until a soft dough forms.

3. Assemble the Fig Newtons:
    - Divide the dough in half. Place one half of the dough between two sheets of parchment paper and roll it out into a rectangle about 1/4 inch thick.
    - Spread half of the fig filling evenly over the rolled-out dough, leaving a small border around the edges.
    - Carefully roll up the dough, jelly-roll style, using the parchment paper to help lift and roll.
    - Repeat the process with the remaining dough and fig filling.
4. Chill the Dough Logs:
    - Wrap the dough logs in plastic wrap and chill them in the refrigerator for at least 1 hour, or until firm.
5. Preheat the Oven:
    - Preheat your oven to 350°F (175°C). Line baking sheets with parchment paper.
6. Slice and Bake:
    - Once the dough logs are chilled, remove them from the refrigerator and unwrap them.
    - Use a sharp knife to slice the dough logs into 1-inch pieces. Place the slices on the prepared baking sheets, spacing them about 1 inch apart.
    - Bake in the preheated oven for 12 to 15 minutes, or until the cookies are golden brown.
7. Cool and Serve:
    - Remove the Fig Newtons from the oven and let them cool on the baking sheets for a few minutes before transferring them to wire racks to cool completely.
    - Enjoy these delicious homemade Fig Newtons as a sweet snack or treat!

These homemade Fig Newtons are soft, chewy, and filled with a flavorful fig filling.

They're perfect for enjoying with a cup of tea or coffee, and they're sure to be a hit with family and friends!

Apple Turnovers

Ingredients:

For the pastry:

- 2 cups all-purpose flour
- 1/2 teaspoon salt
- 2/3 cup unsalted butter, cold and cut into small cubes
- 4-6 tablespoons ice water

For the apple filling:

- 3-4 medium-sized apples, peeled, cored, and diced
- 1/4 cup granulated sugar
- 1 teaspoon ground cinnamon
- 1/4 teaspoon ground nutmeg
- 1 tablespoon lemon juice
- 2 tablespoons unsalted butter
- 2 tablespoons all-purpose flour

For assembly:

- 1 large egg, beaten (for egg wash)
- 2 tablespoons granulated sugar (for sprinkling)

Instructions:

1. Prepare the Pastry:
    - In a large mixing bowl, whisk together the flour and salt.
    - Add the cold, cubed butter to the flour mixture. Use a pastry cutter or your fingers to cut the butter into the flour until the mixture resembles coarse crumbs.
    - Gradually add the ice water, 1 tablespoon at a time, mixing with a fork until the dough starts to come together. Be careful not to overmix.
    - Gather the dough into a ball, flatten it into a disc, wrap it in plastic wrap, and refrigerate for at least 30 minutes.

2. Make the Apple Filling:
   - In a saucepan over medium heat, melt the butter. Add the diced apples and cook until they begin to soften, about 5 minutes.
   - Stir in the granulated sugar, ground cinnamon, ground nutmeg, and lemon juice.
   - Sprinkle the flour over the apple mixture and stir until the mixture thickens slightly, about 1-2 minutes.
   - Remove from heat and let the filling cool completely.
3. Preheat the Oven:
   - Preheat your oven to 375°F (190°C). Line a baking sheet with parchment paper.
4. Assemble the Turnovers:
   - On a lightly floured surface, roll out the chilled pastry dough into a large rectangle, about 1/8 inch thick.
   - Use a sharp knife or pastry cutter to cut the dough into squares or rectangles, depending on the size of turnovers you prefer.
   - Place a spoonful of the cooled apple filling in the center of each dough square or rectangle.
   - Fold one corner of the dough over the filling to the opposite corner, forming a triangle. Press the edges firmly to seal.
5. Bake the Turnovers:
   - Transfer the assembled turnovers to the prepared baking sheet.
   - Brush the tops of the turnovers with beaten egg and sprinkle with granulated sugar.
   - Bake in the preheated oven for 20-25 minutes, or until the turnovers are golden brown and crispy.
6. Cool and Serve:
   - Remove the turnovers from the oven and let them cool on the baking sheet for a few minutes before transferring them to a wire rack to cool completely.
   - Serve the apple turnovers warm or at room temperature, and enjoy!

These homemade apple turnovers are flaky, filled with warm, cinnamon-spiced apples, and perfect for breakfast or dessert. They're sure to be a hit with family and friends!

Chocolate Soufflé

Ingredients:

- 4 ounces (115g) semisweet or bittersweet chocolate, chopped
- 3 tablespoons unsalted butter, plus extra for greasing ramekins
- 1/4 cup granulated sugar, plus extra for coating ramekins
- 3 large eggs, separated
- 1/8 teaspoon cream of tartar (optional)
- 1/4 teaspoon vanilla extract
- Pinch of salt
- Powdered sugar, for dusting (optional)

Instructions:

1. Preheat the Oven and Prepare Ramekins:
    - Preheat your oven to 375°F (190°C). Grease the bottoms and sides of four 6-ounce ramekins with butter. Dust the insides of the ramekins with granulated sugar, tapping out any excess sugar.
2. Melt Chocolate and Butter:
    - In a heatproof bowl set over a pot of simmering water (double boiler), melt the chocolate and butter together, stirring occasionally until smooth. Alternatively, you can melt them in the microwave in short bursts, stirring in between each burst.
3. Prepare the Soufflé Batter:
    - In a large mixing bowl, whisk together the egg yolks and granulated sugar until pale and thickened. Stir in the vanilla extract.
    - Gradually pour the melted chocolate mixture into the egg yolk mixture, stirring until well combined.
4. Whip Egg Whites:
    - In a separate clean, dry mixing bowl, beat the egg whites with a pinch of salt and cream of tartar (if using) until stiff peaks form.
5. Fold Egg Whites into Chocolate Mixture:
    - Gently fold about one-third of the beaten egg whites into the chocolate mixture to lighten it.
    - Carefully fold in the remaining egg whites until no streaks remain, being careful not to deflate the mixture.
6. Fill and Bake the Soufflés:

- Divide the soufflé batter evenly among the prepared ramekins, filling each about three-quarters full.
- Run your thumb around the inside rim of each ramekin to create a slight indentation, which will help the soufflés rise evenly.
- Place the ramekins on a baking sheet and transfer to the preheated oven.
- Bake for 12-15 minutes, or until the soufflés are puffed up and set on top but still slightly jiggly in the center.

7. Serve Immediately:
    - Dust the tops of the soufflés with powdered sugar, if desired.
    - Serve the chocolate soufflés immediately, as they will begin to deflate once they come out of the oven.
    - Enjoy the light, airy texture and rich chocolate flavor of these classic chocolate soufflés as a delightful dessert!

Remember, while soufflés are best served immediately, they're still delicious even if they deflate a bit. So don't worry too much about perfection—just enjoy the process and the delicious results!

Bourbon Pecan Tarts

Ingredients:

For the tart crust:

- 1 and 1/4 cups all-purpose flour
- 1/2 teaspoon salt
- 1/2 cup unsalted butter, cold and cubed
- 2-3 tablespoons ice water

For the filling:

- 1 cup pecan halves
- 1/2 cup granulated sugar
- 1/4 cup light corn syrup
- 2 tablespoons unsalted butter, melted
- 1 tablespoon bourbon
- 1 teaspoon vanilla extract
- 1 large egg, lightly beaten

Instructions:

1. Prepare the Tart Crust:
    - In a food processor, combine the flour and salt. Add the cold, cubed butter and pulse until the mixture resembles coarse crumbs.
    - Gradually add the ice water, 1 tablespoon at a time, pulsing until the dough comes together.
    - Turn the dough out onto a lightly floured surface and shape it into a disk. Wrap it in plastic wrap and refrigerate for at least 30 minutes.
2. Preheat the Oven and Prepare Tart Pans:
    - Preheat your oven to 375°F (190°C). Grease or lightly butter eight 4-inch tart pans.
3. Roll out the Tart Crust:
    - On a lightly floured surface, roll out the chilled dough to about 1/8-inch thickness.
    - Cut out circles of dough slightly larger than the tart pans.

- Gently press the dough circles into the tart pans, trimming any excess dough from the edges. Prick the bottoms of the crusts with a fork.
4. Prepare the Pecan Filling:
    - In a mixing bowl, combine the pecan halves, granulated sugar, light corn syrup, melted butter, bourbon, vanilla extract, and beaten egg. Mix until well combined.
5. Fill the Tart Crusts:
    - Divide the pecan filling evenly among the prepared tart crusts, filling each about three-quarters full.
6. Bake the Tarts:
    - Place the filled tart pans on a baking sheet and transfer to the preheated oven.
    - Bake for 20-25 minutes, or until the filling is set and the crusts are golden brown.
7. Cool and Serve:
    - Remove the bourbon pecan tarts from the oven and let them cool in the tart pans for a few minutes.
    - Carefully remove the tarts from the pans and transfer them to a wire rack to cool completely.
    - Serve the bourbon pecan tarts at room temperature, optionally with a dollop of whipped cream or a scoop of vanilla ice cream.

These bourbon pecan tarts are rich, nutty, and slightly boozy, making them a perfect dessert for special occasions or holiday gatherings. Enjoy the delicious combination of pecans, bourbon, and buttery crust in every bite!

Cherry Bakewell Tart

Ingredients:

For the pastry:

- 1 and 1/4 cups all-purpose flour
- 1/2 cup unsalted butter, cold and cubed
- 1/4 cup granulated sugar
- 1 large egg yolk
- 1-2 tablespoons cold water

For the almond filling:

- 1 cup almond flour or ground almonds
- 1/2 cup granulated sugar
- 1/4 cup unsalted butter, softened
- 1 large egg
- 1 teaspoon almond extract

For the tart:

- 1/2 cup cherry jam or preserves
- 1/4 cup sliced almonds
- Confectioners' sugar, for dusting

Instructions:

1. Make the Pastry:
    - In a food processor, pulse together the flour and cold, cubed butter until the mixture resembles breadcrumbs.
    - Add the granulated sugar and pulse to combine.
    - Add the egg yolk and 1 tablespoon of cold water, and pulse until the dough comes together. Add more water if needed.
    - Turn the dough out onto a lightly floured surface and knead it briefly until smooth.
    - Wrap the dough in plastic wrap and refrigerate for at least 30 minutes.
2. Preheat the Oven and Prepare the Tart Pan:
    - Preheat your oven to 350°F (175°C). Grease a 9-inch tart pan with a removable bottom.

3. Roll out the Pastry:
    - On a lightly floured surface, roll out the chilled pastry dough to fit the tart pan. Line the tart pan with the pastry dough, pressing it into the bottom and sides. Trim any excess dough.
4. Make the Almond Filling:
    - In a mixing bowl, combine the almond flour (or ground almonds), granulated sugar, softened butter, egg, and almond extract. Mix until smooth and well combined.
5. Assemble the Tart:
    - Spread the cherry jam or preserves evenly over the bottom of the pastry-lined tart pan.
    - Spoon the almond filling over the cherry jam, spreading it out evenly.
    - Sprinkle the sliced almonds over the top of the almond filling.
6. Bake the Tart:
    - Place the assembled tart on a baking sheet and transfer it to the preheated oven.
    - Bake for 30-35 minutes, or until the pastry is golden brown and the almond filling is set.
7. Cool and Serve:
    - Remove the tart from the oven and let it cool in the tart pan for a few minutes.
    - Carefully remove the tart from the pan and transfer it to a wire rack to cool completely.
    - Dust the cooled tart with confectioners' sugar before serving.

Enjoy the delightful flavors of almond and cherry in this classic Cherry Bakewell Tart! It's perfect for afternoon tea or as a dessert for any occasion.

Buttermilk Pie

Ingredients:

For the pie crust:

- 1 9-inch pie crust, homemade or store-bought (unbaked)

For the filling:

- 1 and 1/2 cups granulated sugar
- 3 tablespoons all-purpose flour
- 1/2 cup unsalted butter, melted and cooled slightly
- 3 large eggs
- 1 cup buttermilk
- 1 teaspoon vanilla extract
- 1 tablespoon lemon juice
- Zest of 1 lemon (optional)
- Pinch of salt

Instructions:

1. Preheat the Oven and Prepare the Pie Crust:
    - Preheat your oven to 350°F (175°C). Place the unbaked pie crust in a 9-inch pie dish and crimp the edges as desired.
2. Make the Filling:
    - In a large mixing bowl, whisk together the granulated sugar and flour until well combined.
    - Add the melted butter and whisk until smooth.
    - Add the eggs, one at a time, whisking well after each addition.
    - Whisk in the buttermilk, vanilla extract, lemon juice, lemon zest (if using), and a pinch of salt until the filling is smooth and well combined.
3. Pour the Filling into the Pie Crust:
    - Pour the buttermilk filling into the unbaked pie crust, spreading it out evenly.
4. Bake the Pie:
    - Place the pie in the preheated oven and bake for 45 to 50 minutes, or until the filling is set and the top is golden brown. The center may still jiggle slightly, but it will firm up as it cools.

5. Cool and Serve:
    - Remove the pie from the oven and let it cool completely on a wire rack before slicing and serving.
    - Serve slices of buttermilk pie at room temperature or chilled, optionally topped with whipped cream or a dusting of powdered sugar.

Enjoy the rich, creamy texture and sweet flavor of this classic Southern buttermilk pie! It's perfect for any occasion, from holiday gatherings to simple weeknight desserts.

www.ingramcontent.com/pod-product-compliance
Lightning Source LLC
LaVergne TN
LVHW061938070526
838199LV00060B/3860